I0198999

THE GREATEST ESCAPE

By Samuel Quigley
and
Sophia Freda Quigley (nee Rohl)

First published in the United Kingdom in 2023.
Copyright © Samuel/Freda Quigley and family.
All rights reserved.

No part of this book may be reproduced, stored in a retrieval system or transmitted by any other means without prior and express written permission by the author/publisher.

A catalogue record of this book is available from the British Library.

ISBN 978-1-7398258-5-0

Cover © Quigley

Published by © Newford Publishing

This is a true story, a remarkable story, an inspirational story and a story that had to be told in the right way by the right people.

This is Samuel's and Freda's story of how love can overcome even the most difficult challenges. It is also a story of never giving up and believing in what you want in life and, more importantly: who you want in your life.

Samuel and Freda, with the help of their lovely family, have helped to capture the hearts of many people with their amazing war-time diaries. It is with the greatest pleasure that you are about to read the essence of those diaries that are sure to fill your hearts with gasping awe and a warm, loving feeling of a happy ever after.

It is a real-life account of two young people in love during the Second World War. Samuel was a soldier from Northern Ireland who was captured by the Germans and thrown in a prisoner-of-war camp. Freda was a humble German farm girl. Their paths crossed in the most bizarre and surreal circumstances during the conflict. Samuel's promise to Freda that he would whisk her off back home to Northern Ireland once he is free from the clutches of the German guards was not some flawed and skewed promise. He did escape, and he did indeed carry Freda off through the night and into the arms of freedom where they set up home started a family, as promised, in Northern Ireland.

Thanks to Sam and Freda's daughters, Jean & Pamela, for transcribing their story.

INTRODUCTION

There have been many incredible stories originating from the horrors of war. There are great acts of bravery, tragedy, and aching sadness. There are also many great stories of unique experiences, and in the case of Sam and Sophia Freda Quigley — a truly remarkable love story.

This love story is not your typical boy meets girl, and they ride off into the sunset. No, this love story has everything fit for a movie.

This is the true story of a Prisoner of War soldier from Northern Ireland and a poor farm girl from Germany.

The Second World War would bring them both together. Despite everything against them and thrown at them, their love for each other knew no bounds.

This story is a testament to the real human spirit and tenacity. It proves beyond any reasonable doubt that love does indeed conquer all, as Samuel Quigley and Sophia Freda have shown.

Samuel Quigley

When a young Sam Quigley from Muckamore, Co. Antrim, joined the 2nd Battalion Irish Guards, little did he know he would find himself being held captive by the Germans.

What Sam and many, many others hadn't seen coming was the incredible journey ahead. His journey — and that of many others — was one you'd expect from a harrowing Hollywood war movie full of death, torture, pain, starvation, devastation, and destruction.

But there was no movie set and, indeed, no props. After fierce battles in Boulogne, Sam became a Prisoner of War that took him on the most incredible journey no human being should ever have to suffer.

Sam and his Prisoner of War compatriots were forced to prepare mass graves to bury French and Belgian natives who were killed in the conflict; before marching the long, energy and soul-sapping roads to Belgium.

Sadly, not every soldier made it to Belgium. Many injured and sick casualties of war died on their travels. This would cause further distress to the marching survivors.

Their journey would not end there. This was only the beginning. Another painstaking, spirit-crushing and physically-wrecking voyage was upon the Battalion.

Arriving in the town of Bertrix, the tired soldiers were crammed onto cattle trucks. Many of the group had fallen ill with dysentery and had succumbed to other ailments. The depleted squad, all bundled and huddled, were taken to Szubin, a town in occupied Poland. The treacherous journey lasted several days.

Hardship and hard labour were the order of the day as the

Prisoners of War built their own camp.

Samuel Quigley came from humble origins, where his family worked hard in the textile industry and often worked the land around their local rural area.

In 1939 he joined the Irish Guards, where he would go on to serve in the middle east (Palestine and Egypt, respectively).

Samuel Quigley

Date of Birth: 11th May 1919
Date of Death: 12th November 1995

Sophia Freda Quigley (nee Rohl)

Sophia Freda Rohl was a 15-year-old teenage girl when the Second World War was declared. Her family lived very near to the Polish border, and at the time of German soldiers invading Poland, her family were regarded and P-tagged as Polish nationals as they couldn't provide the necessary papers to prove their German nationalities. Sophia Freda and her family were classed as refugees - in the country they were born.

As if things could not get any worse, the family were carted away in cattle trucks to work in various farmlands but they never stayed together as a family unit. They were split and it would take a handful of summers and winters before they would see each other again.

They would reunite at a working farm near Wolfshagen. It would take some time, but the family were officially granted and presented with their German citizenship papers.

Sophia Freda (or Freda as she preferred to be referred to) had a close relationship with her siblings but she had a terribly tough time at the abusive hands of her stepfather.

Life was not kind to the young German girl. War had ravaged her country; she suffered hardship, abuse, and close encounters with a Russian soldier who made his intentions clear in an attempted attack that, thankfully, she escaped from. Freda also survived a bullet that whizzed through her hair.

Her prince, Samuel Quigley, would rescue her with a promise to whisk her home to Northern Ireland. It was a promise he kept and delivered.

In a scene not too far removed from the classic film The Great Escape, Sam would escape from the prison camp he was held captive in, rescue his princess Freda and embarked on the long journey home to safety in Northern Ireland.

Sam and Freda would settle and raise a family of six. Their story is captivating, to say the least.

Sophia Freda Quigley

Date of Birth: 21st December 1925
Date of Death: 2nd July 2011

MY EXPERIENCES IN HOLLAND AND FRANCE, AND, AS A PRISONER OF WAR IN GERMANY

Samuel Quigley

In May 1940, I was part of a consignment of troops sent to France to fight a rear guard action to stall the German Army so that the British `E' Forces could withdraw as France was about to fall.

On 23rd May 1940, we arrived in Boulogne Harbour to find the place in a mess. Soldiers' uniforms, Air Force uniforms, and transport of every kind abandoned; and five boat loads of troops ready to pull out of the harbour. And here were a few Irish Guards and Welsh Guards going in to take on the might of the German Army who had swept through France and Belgium in a few days.

The French had capitulated before the Germans even began their invasion, and for the Belgians, they let the Germans in and then cried for help. If the French and Belgians could not stop the German Army, how could our little force of ill-equipped men stop the Germans? In a few days, the whole of France fell, and I became a Prisoner of War in German hands.

We were rounded up and disarmed. Our first task was to bury the dead. I helped to bury two hundred Belgium and French soldiers in a mass grave outside Boulogne. We never even got time to get their identity. They were just pitched into a mass grave which in the end looked like a large mound. We put a wooden cross and a French and Belgian helmet on top of the grave, and then we were put on the march with millions of French and Belgian prisoners and after marching all day, we were hoarded into fields and guarded by thousands of German guards.

By this time we were very tired and hungry, and the Germans had not much to eat, so we had to scrounge whatever we could so as to survive. I ate raw potatoes and sugar beet. The French and Belgians seemed to have plenty of food, and the farmers en route used to sell their butter and other products to passing prisoners. Still, we had no French money, so we adopted the strong-arm tactics and took it, only to receive the consequences from the German guards. We were so desperate we ate whatever we got. We were so thirsty at times when we were on the march, that we actually drank cows' urine. We used to raid French houses on the way in search of food and drink. We upturned milk carts and scooped up the milk from the road with our steel helmets and drank it.

The Germans used to batter us with rifle butts. I witnessed Warrant Officers and officers from the Ox & Bucks Regiment skinning a dog and cooking it. Two of my Irish Guard comrades caught a small pig and carried it for over a week before they cooked it barbecue style and ate it.

A squad of German prisoners were passing our column, and they chucked packets of Lloyds cigarettes over to us, which were shared out among my comrades. By this time, we were over twenty days on the march and many of the prisoners had either died or had been left to die.

We arrived at Luxembourg and then headed on to a small place called Bertrix, there we crowded into cattle trucks. There were fifty-four men to a wagon and very little space for each person. We remained there for a day with little ventilation. Many in the wagon had dysentery and could not stand up. Others were too weak to walk and were carried away by the German Red Cross personnel.

The journey took four days and we stopped again at Bremmer Haffen Railway Station, where all the sick were again sorted out.

I was picked out because the Germans picked tall men to carry the sick to the ambulance. When I was at the ambulance on one occasion, a bystander called out in English, "Englander Cigaretten!" When I reached for the cigarette, the Gestapo arrested the German who offered it to me, and took him away.

At the end of our journey, we arrived at a place called Schubin 21B, which I believe was in Poland. Many of my comrades were so exhausted they didn't care what happened to them. We were marched to Stalag 21B camp, which had no huts, but marquees. These were in very cramped conditions. We were so tired and weak, we didn't take time to sit down; we just flopped down and lay where we fell. We hadn't even the strength to pull ourselves up, and some of the men died, but because we were determined to survive, we thought of number one, and that was the order of the day.

The food in this camp consisted of the following:

Breakfast	—	Barley Soup
Dinner	—	Pea Soup
Supper	—	1/5 of a loaf of black bread

At this time, we were not receiving any Red Cross parcels until Christmas 1940. When we did get some parcels, there was not enough to go around. We only got one parcel between five men, and the winter of 1940 was very cold. Many men suffered frostbite to their ears and feet, and only for the Polish community giving us some food (putting their own lives at risk) we would have died.

When morning came, we were assembled in the square, counted and put into sections. I was in Number Six Section, which was pretty far back in the queue for grub which wasn't plentiful. We queued up for water soup and bread and had to double for more which we hid. We collected four loaves of German bread which looked like a house brick but tasted nice and fresh. There were also rotten potatoes and soup, which was made with anything the Germans could muster to put into it. Whatever was put into the soup, it went down well because we were hungry and were glad of it. We just thanked God we were alive. A man named Thompson lay next to me in the tent with a ground sheet over his head.

Nobody realised it, but he was dead and had been for about four days.

There were two hundred men in a Company and each morning we were put into sections, twenty men to ten sections consisting of French, Belgian, British, Indian and Polish. The French and Belgians had money, but many of the British had nothing, so we couldn't buy anything from the canteen, so we had to use other tactics.

We were assembled and counted, morning, noon and night and when the numbers were correct, Polish Army biscuits were issued, two and a half biscuits per man. I was chosen to dish them out to each man in my section, and I had to be exact with each half biscuit when it was halved, or I was in trouble. I had to cut the biscuit with my army-issue knife, and I remember cutting the biscuit when the knife slipped and cut my knee. I still have a scar on my knee to the present day. The Polish biscuits were like bricks, they were very hard, and we needed good teeth to eat them. Some of the prisoners who couldn't eat them would have dipped them into water or make-shift coffee to soften them.

We had a Company Sergeant Major named Tringe who was in charge of our squad and belonged to the Cheshire Regiment. He used to dish up our dinner out of a large boiler. The potatoes were kept separate in a large wooden box. As we were always at the back of the queue, the food was very low by the time it came to our turn to be served. We would stampede to the front and the Sergeant Major used to end up with his head in the boiler of soup as he wasn't serving the food out fairly. My comrade, Cassidy and I used to raid the cookhouse each morning to get some potatoes. When the potatoes started to boil in the large boilers, the cookhouse would get steamed up so much, the Germans couldn't see us making our raid, but many times we got caught and flogged for it. The canteen would open each morning for those with money who could buy bread, jam and cakes, and as we British had no money, we had to put our plan into action. We would place one of our comrades among the onlookers who were watching the bread and cakes being carried into the canteen. I would have my hands full of bread and my comrade would snatch a few loaves from my arms and make a run for it. We had to do things like this if we were to survive, but if we got caught by the German guards we suffered the consequences at the end of the rifle butt.

During the day, there wasn't much to do as there were thousands of prisoners and all of them could not be employed building the camp, so we would lounge about waiting for the next meal. Cassidy and I would take a walk to the back of the cookhouse, where we might get a ladle of soup which contained bones from horses, etc, but it tasted alright because we were so hungry. We would raid the store which contained the Polish Army biscuits and again we would be chased by the guards. We used to throw the biscuits into a communal toilet and when things quietened down, we would go back to the toilet and get the biscuits out, wash and eat them.

When we were registered as Prisoners of War, we would make contact with the Poles and barter our army boots and clothes with them for bread and homegrown tobacco. The Germans would have to re-clothe us with Polish Army uniforms and send us out in working parties outside the camp in the morning and return at night. The Poles used to risk their lives to give us something to eat, and when they were caught they would suffer.

After a few months, when we were sorted out, I was sent with a party to work on a building site in a small town called Znin in Poland, and the Germans named it Dietford. First, we were making a communal park and then in the town, a market place and a cinema. I was working on the new cinema which the Germans called The Bismark. On the day it was ready to open we gave the Germans a treat by catching all the fleas in our camp and placing them in matchboxes and jars; then we let them loose in the cinema. We also stole jars of coffee, took the coffee out, fill the jars with sawdust and sprinkle some coffee on top and put the lids on again.

Instead of a jar of coffee, we had left a jar of sawdust for the Germans.

We were paid German Marks for our work in the camp which was useless outside the camp. When the Germans opened a canteen inside the camp, we had to queue up at 3am (the canteen opened at 6am) to get a loaf of bread and then we had to queue up for our barley soup and then off to work, collect our tools (hammers, spades, shovels, etc.) We would then head off for a communal toilet which consisted of a trench in the ground surrounded by timber to conceal us from the public. We went to this toilet first thing in the morning to hear the propaganda about the war. We would bury some of our tools in the toilet and when we had finished work for the day, the tools were collected and counted by the Germans. There were so many short the German officer picked another man called Morris and myself for sabotage and laid into us with rifle butts and sent us in front of a German General who was in our area prior to the invasion of Russia in 1941. The German General told me that he was a Prisoner of War during the 1914-1918 War in Manchester and said he was in hospital and was well treated. He gave Morris and me some German sausage and some bread but stopped our ration of beer for a week. We were getting no beer rations anyway.

<u>1941</u>

When the Germans entered the War in June 1941 against Russia, we were moved from Poland into Mariainburge in Prussia, and then we were sorted out. I went on a working party which consisted of twenty-five men and we were sent to a place called Lakendurph near Danzig and Elbing (a farming community).

During the summer we helped with the hay and harvest.

In the winter, we worked on a new bridge over a canal, but it was never a success during the time I was there.

Firstly, we were put to work on a bridge-building job over a canal. Our job was to fill in each end of the bridge with soil, but as we started this in the winter of 1941, the weather was so severe the soil which we had emptied at each end of the bridge froze up and gave way. Then when the thaw came it gave way completely and the whole thing collapsed and it was scrapped. We had two zinc boats at this job and the owner of the boats wanted them back before the thaw came, so we went about to relieve these boats from the frozen water with pick axes and in the process, we damaged the bottom of the boats.

When we were taking these boats back up the canal, they began to let in water, and our German guards could not swim, so we let them sit in the boats until the water was near their waist, and then we rescued them; by which time they were beginning to panic.

During the winter of 1941, we then only worked cutting

timber for local people, and each morning we would line up outside our camp and the Germans would pick the men who they wanted. They always picked tall men, so a chap called Drury and me were picked to fell trees for a woman who, in turn, fed us and paid the German guards for our work. The person whom I worked for had two children and over time she told me that she had fallen in love with me and gave me the key to her house and asked me to break out of the camp at night to see her. To break out of camp was nearly impossible, as the German guards lived in the house close to the camp, so I had a task to perform which wasn't easy. The windows had iron bars across them at the back and front of the building, but at the back window where the toilet was situated, there was a window pane measuring fifteen inches square, and it opened out like a door. So I started to concentrate on how to get out of it as a prisoner at another camp showed me how to squeeze through such a small space. I put this into operation, and it worked.

I did not want the other prisoners to know that I was breaking out of the camp at night and returning before daylight in time for the roll call, so I waited until everyone was asleep before I moved.

This went on for eighteen months before any of the other prisoners realised I was seeing a woman at night and returning in the morning. If I had been caught, the penalty was that I'd be shot as I was seeing a German woman.

I moved away from the window escape route to the roof of the building. I cut a hole in the roof close to some pipes. This building used to be an old creamery and the pipes came in handy for climbing up. I got an old jam tin and cut a piece the size of the hole in the roof, painted the piece of tin white which was the same colour as the roof and replaced this piece of tin every morning when I came in. I never went out every night, only three nights a week, but through time I gave this up and tried a window above my bed, which had a part at the top which opened out. There was a snag here as there were iron bars the full length of the window, but I overcame this by sawing the iron bar close to the base with a hack saw blade (this took me about six hours) and on doing this, I nearly lost my forefinger as the blade slipped and nearly cut me to the bone. I managed it but it took me some time. I removed the bit of bar at the base and worked on the other part until I made it loose enough and placed a saddle spring to make it firm at the top and flush at the bottom. After I removed the piece at the bottom, it was solid, and when I wanted out, I would prise the bar upwards and lift it out of the socket at the bottom, allowing me to get out at the top part of the window. This was OK for a long time, but another chap in our camp was a locksmith in civilian life, and we had a back door on this building, so I began to concentrate on this as another escape route. Another prisoner had also met a partner, and it was a bit awkward to go through the window, so I went for the door. I had to get an impression of the key of the back door, so every Sunday morning when we drew items out of our Red Cross parcels, I would take notice of the key, got a bar of soap and took an impression and gave it to this chap to cut me a key. By this time, more of the prisoners were finding themselves partners and were always asking me to help them to get out. I helped them and one night, my comrade and myself were planning to go out to see our girlfriends as they both lived close to each other. We were holding a conversation and had planned our way out to meet the girls. When the time came for us to go out, we walked through the door with no bother, we then climbed onto the flat roof and were just about to let ourselves down to the ground when one of the guards appeared, and I had to hoist myself up onto the roof again and wait for a while. My partner then lowered himself and I followed suit.

When we got to the front of the building, we were confronted with two German guards with rifles ready to shoot us, but they asked us questions as to where we got out and who we were seeing and we said were going to a Polish Community dance. These two German guards were being transferred to France shortly and they told us to get back into camp and no further action would be taken against us provided we would not say anything to the other prisoners as to what had happened. So we promised not to say a word. Some time afterwards, before the two guards were leaving for France, they told us we had an informer in our midst who had told the owner of the guest house (where the guards used to visit at night) that some prisoners were breaking out of the camp at night. This informer (also a prisoner) had a Polish girlfriend who worked at the guest house and he was unable to see her because of the presence of the guards.

I was working for a Burgermeister at this time, and a chap from the Southampton area (who got a job on a farm next to where I worked) asked me to arrange a date with a girl for him, but when time came for him to break out of the camp, he took cold feet. I had to break out of camp and explain to the girl what had happened.

In doing so, my girlfriend spotted me talking to this other girl, and she dumped me there and then. I didn't really mind because my relationship with her was purely a friendly one and nothing more, as her mother lived with her in the same house. To be truthful, food and cigarettes were my main reasons for going to see her. A chap called Ellis, who came from the Yorkshire area, used to keep me informed about her as he worked on a farm close to where she lived, but things were never the same for me, and she blamed me for two-timing her, so that was the end of our relationship.

One Sunday morning in 1941, while the Germans were taking a roll call of the prisoners, we noticed a Polish chap outside our camp making signs with his arms. We asked our interpreter what was going on, but he was unable to tell us what the Pole meant. During the evening, a chap named Pearson who worked in the guard-room noticed Hesse's picture was missing from the wall. We realised that was what the Polish chap was trying to tell us when he was making signs with his arms as if he was playing the bagpipes and Hesse was in Scotland and the Germans did not know at this time.

After this escapade, we were sent to work on small farms during the summer of 1942, helping with the hay and then the harvest, but we did not get fed by the farmers at this time, so we filled our pockets with wheat and brought it back to the camp. We ground it and made a sort of porridge which staved off the hunger until our Red Cross parcels started to arrive.

1942

During the winter of 1942, there was not much work on the farms, so many of us lined up in the morning for roll call, and some of the local people, namely old German pensioners, would ask the German guards for a couple of prisoners to fell trees for firewood during the winter. As I said, these people always picked tall men to work for them, so Drury and myself always got the jobs. When we first came to this camp the beds were made up with straw, but the French prisoners had been there before us, and they and the beds were dirty, so we got rid of the straw and lay on the bare boards. An old lady kept pigs in a shed close to our camp, and she took the straw for her pigs. After a short time, she complained that the straw was full of fleas and that the English fleas bite, but the German fleas don't. I told her that the fleas were French.

We took some trees down for this old lady, who made troughs out of the butt of the tree and used this to salt the pigs in when they were killed. The pigs took swine fever and the old lady asked me to shoot them. I told her that I had no gun, only an axe, so I didn't get killing her pigs. The farmers asked us to kill pigs for their own use but the German authorities did not know about this, for if they did, the farmers would have been shot or imprisoned, so when we helped with this matter, we got a piece of pig for ourselves.

Many of the people around our area were not proper Germans and treated us well. There were Poles working on the state farms, and some of the prisoners got to know some of the girls on the farms and had relationships with them. If the soldiers were caught with these girls, they were severely punished. I remember one chap who came to me and asked me if I could get him out of the camp to see his Polish girlfriend. I said I would, so I helped him out one night after roll call, and the next morning he told me that when he was outside the building his great coat had disappeared.

I said that the guard must have found it and told him to stay behind and clean the place up, and ask the guard if he had seen the coat. The guard said he had, so the chap said he was going to escape. He had with him chocolate, soap and an alarm clock in the pocket of the great coat. By this time, we had a few of the younger German guards in charge and we were about to be sent to the West Wall in France, so they didn't care and did nothing about the matter.

When new guards took over, we had to lie low to watch their movements at night, and there was a guest house nearby that the guards used to frequent at night. We would break out when the guards got drunk, and we knew the road was clear.

During our stay in Dietford in Poland in the winter of 1940/41, things were pretty tough and we had very little to eat (only barley soup and one-fifth of a German loaf which wasn't much to keep us alive).

We had to depend on our Polish friends, who risked their lives by sharing their food with us. If they were caught doing so, they were severely punished. I remember helping a Polish roofer in the hotel when I noticed a Polish woman hiding some food for the prisoners beside a large stone, and I collected this food and shared it with my comrades.

This was carried out each morning for some time, and then it stopped.

I found out later why it had stopped, the reason being that our German guard had spotted the Polish woman placing the food parcel beside the stone, so the guard approached her one morning and tried to make a date with her. The next morning when she turned up to place the parcel at the stone the German Police arrested her. The reason she was arrested was because she didn't turn up for the date with the guard and the so-called German policeman was not really a policeman but a Polish man who had signed the papers to become a German at the fall of Poland in 1939.

There were quite a few of them in this Polish town which was occupied by German troops and some of the Polish were worse then the Germans here. The Polish woman got six weeks in jail and was flogged. When she came out of jail, she was soon helping the prisoners again.

In our camp in Dietford, Poland, there was an old sugar beet factory which housed one hundred and fifty-seven prisoners and it was very cold. There were 39 degrees of frost in winter and we couldn't work because of the cold. As we couldn't work we had to go on a route march for miles and because it was so cold with snow and frost, our faces used to freeze up and our nostrils were clogged with ice.

I said that the reason we were taken on this march was because the camp staff who were prisoners preparing our dinner would get the Germans to take us out so as they would get the best things for their dinner and we would get the leftovers. I got into trouble for saying this.

The prisoners in the camp were allocated different jobs. There were about twenty-five men in each party and after breakfast each morning we were marched off to our place of work. I was at one time working in a cellar and my job was to break a huge stone up with another prisoner who was a Scotsman. During a conversation with him, he told me his name was Makenzie and he was serving with the Cameron Highlanders in France when he was captured.

He had come from Australia to join the Camerons as his father was a Sergeant Major in the Regiment during 1914/18 War. He told me he was going to escape and had a Polish guide to help him, and asked me if I would cover up for him when the Germans came to count our numbers. I did this and it worked at the job and at the roll call at camp.

We were locked up for the night and around 3am in the morning, we were awakened by the German guards who ordered us to parade downstairs for the roll to be called as a prisoner had turned up at the gate and said he belonged to our camp but the guard on the gate told him to "piss off" as he had the numbers correct, but when we were counted again, they found one short and we were all punished for this.

When we were going to work in the morning, we passed through a railway station which had a large assignment of coal stacked in it.

Each night when we passed through the railway station most of the prisoners would lift a lump of coal (about a stone in weight) and take it into camp hidden below our great coats and stack it under our bed spaces. By the time the German guards caught on to what we were doing, we had about a ton of coal in each of our billets. The Germans then whitewashed the coal so they could keep a check on the coal stack.

Our prison camp was a mixture of nationalities comprising of Jews, Irish, English, Scots and Welsh. Escape from the camp was almost impossible because of weather conditions and the state of the prisoner's health. A few prisoners tried to escape but were caught shortly afterwards.

Outside our camp was a large boating lake which the Germans

used for boating trips, but in winter it froze over to a depth of over a foot in ice and it did not start to thaw until February, and even then, there were patches of ice spread over the lake.

I remember while we were in the camp during the winter and spring of 1940/1941, some high-ranking German officers came to the lake with their boats to have a boating outing. When they launched their boats and went out into the lake, some of them hit some ice and were in difficulties and their boats sank. A call went out for help, and two or more prisoners who were good swimmers volunteered to go to the German officer's assistance, but our officer in charge would not allow this, so the German officers were all drowned in the lake. At that time, there was a rumour going around that anyone doing a good deed in Germany would be patriated back to England as that was happening to the French prisoners.

We had two medical orderlies in our camp in Poland. One was a Welsh Guards Corporal and the other was a Medical Corps orderly. When we needed medical attention, we used to pay them a visit but they never had much medical kit, but I remember paying them a visit once and I noticed what I thought to be human bones lying around the floor in a small room. I found out afterwards that the Welsh man was working on a Jewish cemetery digging up graves as the Germans were using everything for their war effort. The Welsh man was carrying the bones home to the camp to build a skeleton to study the parts of the body.

The first parcels we received from the Red Cross were at Christmas 1940, but there was not enough to go around, so we split the prisoners into parties of five and cut the cards, and every fifth prisoner got a parcel between them. I remember one prisoner from East Yorkshire getting a share of the parcels, and he ate everything he got, including the soap. He finished up using two toilet buckets as he was very sick.

1944

I remained at the working camp until 1944, when the Germans thought up a scheme and thought the Irish were neutral and called us Irish. We were all taken into a prison camp called Lukenvalda near Berlin, but instead of us cooperating with the Germans, we mutinied, and as a result, I was sent out on a working party to a camp called Wolfshagan. I was housed in an old barn surrounded by barbed wire and guarded with a German sentry at the front and back of the building. Our beds consisted of three-tier beds with no mattresses, only bare board. The food was terrible. We received one Red Cross food parcel each month, and the place was overcrowded and was alive with rats which used to fall from the beams at night onto our beds and then onto the floor where we had a cat called Muggy who caught seven or more rats every day and night.

As the place was so overcrowded, twenty of us complained abut food, housing, etc, and the next thing we knew, the Straff guards arrived and beat us up with their rifle butts and we just rose again and laughed at the Germans until they got fed up but it didn't break our spirits, so they picked eleven men and put us on Straff work and transferred us to another camp called Commernitz where we were housed in an old stable infested with rats as well, but the German guards used to shoot the rats at night with a .22 rifle so we got most of them out of the way. By this time we were getting no Red Cross parcels, so we had to depend on what the Germans gave us for food. There was a huge estate farm and the person who owned it was a high-ranking officer in the German Army called Herr Von Bousie. He was stationed in the Berlin area during this time (July 1944). His wife and daughter were at home and used to give us anything we wanted from the garden. It was help ourselves sort of style. We had tomato soup nearly every day of the week and we worked in the fields with sugar beet, gathering potatoes and cutting cabbage.

The guard would take us out to the land early in the morning and work to dinner time. We went back to the camp for dinner, then back to the fields until night.

The guard was pretty old and smoked the pipe. One day we saw him searching his pocket for tobacco and he couldn't find any (so a pal of mine called Hinds, who got parcels containing War Horse Tobacco sent from his home in Belfast) gave him some. This tobacco is very strong, so we gave the guard a pipe full and got him to take a pull of the pipe. His face turned colour, and we had the rest of the day off as the guard was very sick.

We were set a task every day. We had to plant two very long rows of cabbage and when we had two rows finished we stood up ready to march back to camp when the guard told us to plant another row, but we didn't respond. The guard then raised the rifle to his shoulder and cocked it, but we stood still, and after a while, his nerves got the better of him, and we were marched back to camp.

On Christmas Eve 1944, we had no Red Cross food parcels, so a chap named Roy from Belfast and myself took it upon ourselves to steal goods which were housed in the yard next to the camp, so we cut the barbed wire in two places, got out and arrived at the yard at around 7.30pm with a full moon and nearly a foot of white-crisp snow. When we got near the geese (which were still out in the yard) they raised the alarm and a woman who was dishing out milk reported us to the guards, but we got back in time to camp. There was only one problem, I left part of my trousers on the wire and the German guards found it and were checking everyone to see who had a hole in their trousers but I managed to change as I had two pairs of trousers.

They could not find out who owned the piece of cloth.

At this stage the prisoners were not counted and there were

two men who had broken out to go to the village where the Poles worked as they were promised cakes and buns for Christmas but in the end got none.

The guards came again to call the roll and found out then that there was two men missing as there were supposed to be eleven men in camp and they only counted nine. The alarm was raised at Army Headquarters in Wittenburge, that two English prisoners were missing, so the whole German forces around the area were alerted, so we had a job on our hands to try and get these two men back into camp without the German guards seeing them. We put our plan into action by talking to the guards and keeping them in cigarettes while our two men crawled through the snow and into the camp without being noticed.

When the guard called the roll again later on, the men were present and the German guards were sent to the Russian front. The camp was closed and we were sent back to our camp, where we had originally come from.

1945

In January 1945, we were put to work in the woods cutting timber for pit props. Our task was to cut timber into two meters each day, and a pal of mine from Portavogie (Tom Pyper) worked on a farm and asked me one day if I would like to meet a young girl who worked on the farm. The girl was called Freda, and was a good friend of Tom's girlfriend, who was called Toni. I broke out of camp that night (to go on a 'blind date') and our way out was via an old dry toilet which bordered the barbed wire, half inside the wire and the other half just level with the outside wire, so that was our escape route, again keeping the guard occupied while we got out. We made our bed up so it looked like a body was in it, and as the light wasn't too good inside the camp, the guards used to go around counting and as long as they felt what seemed like a body, it passed. There were 57 men in our camp, and about twenty of them used to go out at night and return before daybreak before the guards had the roll call. The guard on the gate would take some men from the camp up to the yard to collect the coffee for breakfast then we would slip in unnoticed. I started to see Freda often, and realised I was falling in love, and wanted Freda for my wife. I knew the next few months were going to be difficult ones and my mind started working overtime as I thought about a plan to escape.

As I mentioned before, I worked in the woods and my pal Tom worked on the farm where my girlfriend (Freda) worked and one day during the summer of 1944 while bringing in the harvest, we were all sitting down drinking coffee, when Freda's mum brought some fruit to give out to the prisoners. She placed the fruit in Freda's lap and when the German guard asked if he could have some fruit, he grabbed Freda, in turn, Freda came upon the guard's arm with a coffee bottle. During the afternoon while stacking the corn and barley into the loft from the wagon, there was a New Zealander, who was too small to reach the loft. The guard was told to take the New Zealander back to camp and get a taller man to pitch the corn. On the road back to camp, the guard shot the prisoner in the back and said he did so because this was the man who was escaping and had hit the guard on the elbow with a stone. When the truth came out, we found out that the guard had been lying and Freda gave evidence against the guard who was in turn taken out and shot, so Freda's life was in danger after that as was her father and the people who lived in the village, but Freda stuck to her story and I got into trouble with the German guard while working at the timber.

Freda nearly lost her life a day or so before she left home. She was watching her father killing a bullock for the Polish workers, who were making their way home again to Poland. A Russian soldier appeared on the scene and cornered Freda in her own house. He locked all the doors and he was about to try something on, when Freda saw her chance and made her escape through a French bay window. The Russian fired two shots from his revolver, which passed through Freda's hair, but luckily, she managed to escape unhurt.

This wasn't the first encounter Freda had with the Russians. Her father sent her to fetch him some homegrown tobacco from a neighbour and when she mounted her bicycle, four Cossacks on horseback approached and was about to interfere with her when I came on the scene. I probably saved her from being molested. I said that she was mine and they rode off.

There was one chap who was taken prisoner in Italy by the Germans and was working with me in the woods, but he could not understand a word of German. When the guard told him to work harder, he asked me what the guard said, so I told the German guard that when the Russians came, he would get his throat cut, so the guard inspected my work and he found that I had cut the timber into foot lengths instead of two-metre lengths. As this wasn't long enough for pit props, it was used for the fire back at the camp, and I was charged with sabotage and sent to Berlin on the charge by train. As we got as far as Wittenburge, the lines to Berlin were bombed and our trains could not travel, so instead I went with two chaps called Harris and Lindrum to the hospital in Wittenburge where we were given food and cigarettes by wounded German soldiers. We returned to our camp and I made up my mind to escape, as our camp was being evacuated away from the advancing Russian Army, who were then in the Poland borders, and the Germans were getting desperate. I told my pal Tom of my plan to escape, and early in February 1945 we made our bid. Twenty men in all escaped, but the Germans re-captured eighteen of them during that night, but Tom and myself evaded capture and watched the Germans with searchlights all night, trying to capture us, but failed. We were well hidden in a drain, and when it was dawn, we made our way to a hay shed and made our homes there by building bales of hay around us deep in the shed. There, we stayed until the Russians arrived at the end of April. We would appear at night to receive food from Freda and Toni.

We lay in the shed not knowing that an American bomber had been hit by German flak and the bombs were dropping close to our hay shed. We were in the shed for some time when one day we heard rustling in the hay. We went to investigate and found a man hiding in the hay. At first he said he was Russian but then he confessed to being an officer in the German Army. He was armed and soon after that a second officer came and we took a chance when they said they wouldn't harm us. They apparently were running away from the Russian front.

We later heard that S.S. Officers were looking for British prisoners to take their uniforms and try to pass for British Prisoners of War.

One morning nearing the end of April, we saw men throwing things away into a swamp, and a short time later the Russian tanks appeared. We came out of our hiding place and gave ourselves up to the Russians but they didn't understand us, so we went down to the small village of Sedein where we found some clothing; shirts and underwear etc. We were feeling quite lousy with lying in the hay for so long and as we were about to leave the shop, a Russian officer appeared at the trap door pointing a revolver at us because the shopkeeper had said we were plundering. We explained to the Russian officer as best we could that we were British prisoners, and he told us to burn the place. He also warned us to make ourselves ready to get out of the area because when the Russian Controllers came, we would not be able to move.

Tom and I soon made up our minds and told Freda and Toni

our plans. We made ready a wagon which we pinched from a German refugee and took carpet from the Baron's house, which we used to make a cover for the wagon. We filled eight sacks of potatoes and corn for the horses.

We were going to pinch meat from the Germans who had it hidden under a boiler.

At ten o'clock one night at the beginning of May, Tom and Toni arrived at Freda's house. Her father shouted at Freda to put the cat out, and that was when we made our move to escape. I grabbed Freda by the arms and ran. Her father was shouting, "Freda, come back!" but Freda kept on running until we were quite a distance away. I dragged Freda through a sewer and she was covered in slime and gutters to the knees.

Then we went to Toni's place, where Freda got cleaned up, had a rest and at two o'clock the next morning, we made our way through the fields until we found somewhere to hide. We found a whin bush where we hid the two girls. Tom and myself went down to the farm yard and entered the stables and stole two horses. Mine belonged to Freda's father and Tom's belonged to a refugee. We went back to the field to collect Freda and Toni, then made our way back to the yard where we had the wagon. We knocked a German over with the wagon, yoked our horses to the wagon and killed eleven hens and put them in a bag and set off for Pearliburge. On the road we met a large number of Russian armour tanks with men and German prisoners. We kept going until we came to Wittenburge, thinking we could get over the bridge, but the Germans had blown the bridge up, so we were left in the thick of the war.

We travelled approximately 30-40 miles each day, and then bed down for the night. By this time the refugees were joining our wagon trail.

One morning I noticed a party of four on one horse which turned out to be an American soldier who was captured in

Wittenburge by the Germans and had escaped and met a German housewife who was fleeing from the Russians. She had her mother and her daughter with her as well.

They asked if they could join our wagon trail, and we agreed that they could, but we told them we could not feed them as we did not have much for ourselves, so they came along with us too. Our numbers were increasing as we had quite a few women with us.

The Russians were in the area and were molesting the women. We stopped at a place near Dermitz for the night and the Russians called with us looking for women but we had them hidden in a loft above where we were staying.

The old man who owned the place had a boat, so we asked him if he would ferry the women over the Elbe where they would be safe. We gave him share of our food. He agreed to this, so it took a load of our shoulders.

Next morning, we made our way to the town of Dermitz where we were confronted with a squad of American soldiers who wouldn't let us through the town, so we had to find a Russian officer, but we had to drink a toast to Stalin before the Russians would let us go. They came down with us to where the American soldiers were and the Russians had to threaten the Americans with the gun before we were allowed to carry on.

Further on in the journey, we came to a schoolhouse, and the contents consisted of guns, ammunition and army equipment. Tom and I armed ourselves with a German Brit Gun and ammunition and rode escort to our wagon trail of refugees.

Nearby, there was a farmhouse which had nice Italian hens, so we collared one and did the needful, but we had very little cooking utensils so we asked the woman who owned the place to lend us a pot to cook our hen in. She obliged, but in the process, while the hen was being cooked, the woman pinched the giblets, and at the same time, she didn't realise it was her hen that we were cooking. When we had finished our meal, it was time to hit the trail again, so we had a look around the place. We came across a stable full of fresh horses, one being an Arabic horse with two bits in its mouth. It was very sturdy and fresh, as it had been in the stable for some time. My pal Tom worked with horses in Australia before the war and was able to handle horses of any type, so he got on the horse in a very short space of time and had it broken in and fit to ride. We had forty school children plus their teacher in our trail and as we were going into the war zone again, we thought the children would be safer where we were, so we bid them farewell and set off on our journey towards the town of Naus House. On the road, we came across a spearhead of American troops which turned out to be part of the 106 Airborne Division. These were the same outfit as our American friend we had come across at the start of our journey. When he saw his own troops he disappeared and we were left with his woman friend, her mother and daughter to care for.

At long last, we reached the Elbe and Pontoon Bridge over the Elbe was no good for our horse transport, so we had to wait to see what would happen. In the meantime, we were short of food so we decided to do something about it. Nearby there was a field full of cattle, so we took it upon ourselves to shoot a young heifer which we skinned and cut into pieces.

We put some of it into an old German Army field cooker which we had collected along the way. We had some Dutch people in our wagon trail and they did the cooking. When they had the meal cooked, I asked which part of the heifer I was about to eat, and they informed me that it was the lungs. I told my pal that he could have my share.

A short time later, an American General appeared on the

scene and enquired about the heifer we had shot, as they said they had to account for all the livestock, etc. I told them we had lots of people to feed and that this was important. At the same time, I had a hen behind my back ready to be plucked and Freda had milked some cows in a field nearby. This would help us to wash our would-be dinner down.

Our refugee friends were taken away from us then and put in pens. Each nationality were separated so we were clear and were told that we would be ferried over the Elbe by boat during the night, but when the time came we were informed that as the war was not over in this area, we would be going to town next morning where we would get transport to Luneburge. We went to a nearby field where some horses were grazing and picked a couple of nice black ones out which turned out to be very fresh. We found (what we call in Ireland a jaunting car) nearby and yoked a pair of horses into it and set off for the town which was about three miles away. When we arrived in the town, we couldn't get the horses to stop so we made for the nearest field and in the end, we had to run up against a wall to get the horses to stop. Maybe they didn't understand us, as we didn't speak to them in German.

Our transport arrived shortly afterwards, and the convoy consisted of refugees in German Army lorries, German drivers and escorted by American soldiers. I couldn't drive, so Freda and I jumped in beside the German driver in the second wagon in the convoy. My pal got into the first wagon and put the German prisoner into the back of the wagon.

My pal's wagon drove off in a different direction from what we had taken, so I lost my pal.

After driving for a good part of the day, we arrived on the outskirts of the town called Lugwitzlust, but it hadn't fallen, so we were caught in the middle of the battle. A German police officer pulled us into the hallway for safety and gave Freda and me a mug of coffee and a German bread roll.

When the town had surrendered, I reported to the Canadian Army Headquarters and was accommodated in a hotel until the next morning when my wife and I were collected by a person called Captain Young and taken to Luneburge where we were housed by the Second British Army Headquarters.

Here, I met up again with my pal and Australian friend, whom I thought I had lost. I asked him where he was staying and he took me to a place where we stayed for a few days until the landing strip could be repaired, as the Germans had the airstrip ploughed up before surrendering.

During the first night of our stay at this house, we were disturbed by two British officers with two women who tried to move us out of the house and they would take over, but we told them that we were staying where we were, and then they left. We were well looked after in Luneburge by all the staff, and were given clothes and our women folk were catered for as well.

On Monday morning we were told to make ourselves ready for one o'clock (lunchtime) as a plane would fly us to Brussels, where we were to stay until transport was ready to take us to England.

Freda and her friend were taken to Tac H in Brussels where they were to stay until such times as we were taken to England. I got a bit worried about Freda and Toni, so we thought we would pay them a visit where they were staying in this Tac H Hostel. When we arrived there, Freda told us they were being hassled by men trying to get into their cubicles, so we took them from this place and got them accommodation in a hotel in the centre of Brussels. We were catered for by the Army Catering Corps and had very good food, but only men were allowed into the mess. We managed to smuggle our Freda and

Toni in for their meals which was self-service. For breakfast in the hotel, we only had toast and marmalade and coffee. When it was time for us to pay for our stay at the hotel, we paid the landlord in German Marks, which we had found along the way.

A million marks wouldn't buy a loaf of bread then, but we got away with it and were on the road to Croydon Airport where we were kitted out with new clothes.

We then had to leave Freda and Toni, who were then taken to an ATS camp in North London. We were at Croydon Airport until midnight when a Company Sergeant Major of a Scottish Regiment arrived and took me and Tom to Slough Army Camp, where we were bedded down at three o'clock in the morning. After our rest we were taken to the pay office, where I was sorted out, but my pal who was in the Australian Army was not so lucky, as his Army Headquarters as in Margate. We set off to find it, got onto the train at Slough Railway Station, didn't bother to purchase a ticket, changed at Victoria for Margate and still got no tickets. We arrived in Margate at Australian Army Headquarters, but as my pal's papers were still in Australia we made no progress.

We travelled back to London to find Freda and Toni, only to find they had been shifted to another camp and were told by the authorities that if they were not claimed within four days, they would be sent back to where they came from. We found them on Sunday 20th May, and I went to Euston Station hoping to catch the boat for home in Ireland. I was disappointed, the only boat available was from Stranraer to Larne and there was no boat sailing until Monday 21st May. When I arrived I was told by the military police that I would have to sail on the military boat and Freda on the civilian boat, but in the end I joined Freda and arrived home on Monday 21st May 1945.

At the time of writing this, over fifty years has passed and during that time, Freda and I have raised six children, Terry, Jean, Edith, Samuel, Eric and Pamela. They have all left home and between four of them, they have given us twelve grandchildren.

We moved to the small hamlet of Claragh in County Down in 1959, where we still live today.

The War Letters

Original letters from Sam Quigley

I was born in Randalstown on May 1919 and moved to Muckamore village when I was six months old where my Father had obtained work at the Factory known as the York Street Bleaching and Linen Factory Muckamore When I was five years old I started School which was called Island Bawn Public Elementry School the scholars chistened it the Salt Box. School uniforms were unheard of in these days Jerseys, short trousers and stockings and Slippers were worn in Summer and in Winter Cloggs were the footwear and could be rigged out for a couple of Pound Boys and girls wore Cloggs in the Winter and were warm on the feet

There were no such class Rooms in those days we were all in one Class Room Boys & Girls two teachers one Woman teacher and one Man the woman teacher had the children from Infants to 2ND Class and the main teacher had from 3RD to six Class which was the highest in those days and no such thing as Prodestant or Catholic school then we were all mixed together and when we had Religeon instruction once a week for half an Hour Prodestant children had a free break and the same thing happend with th Catolic children and we all got on well Together Religeon was never talked about in there days. I was always at hand after school hours to help many of the pupils who were a bit backward with their home work Our two teachers of our school names were Miss Agnew from Kells who rode a bike to school and Mr Bell also from that area came in a Pony

2

and Irop and the school hours were from 9 a.m. until 3 p.m. with an hour break for lunch from 12 p.m. until 1 p.m. but we had no playground or any facilities in those days except Rounders which was played with a tennis ball, or some used to bring a football to school and play football, but as there was very little space for playground and the ball would break a window then we were in trouble.

In 1929 I met with an bar Accident and was in Hospital for quite some time with head and an Arm injury and was in a Coma for almost two weeks and when I regained conciousness again I got out of bed put my clothes on and was making my way down the corridor on my way home when I met the Surgeon who asked me where I was going I said home and I was ordered back to the ward and bed and found out I had broken some of my stitches on the Arm which had to be repaired again. I spent six weeks in Hospital and then I had to spend some time with a sand bag tied to my arm to try and straighten the arm as it was so long in a sling and it is still not straight to the present day. While I was in hospital I received a card or letter from every pupil and teacher at the school wishing me well again.

When I was ready to start school again our school was closed down and we were all allotted different schools I went to Muckamore Elemtary School where I attended until I was fourteen years of age and reached a good Standard of Education, but there was no work in the early thirties only unskilled jobs so I was put on the waiting list in the factory as my parents had no money to send any of the family to College.

3

So in 1933 I got a job in the factory as a machine Quarter wages and found a week less Insurance Stamp money ten pence leaving Nineteen shilling and two pence to take home, where I received one shilling pocket money to last me a week. Our Boss used to give the workers under him half a Crown a month as he was paid monthly.

I started this job in 1933 and was in constant employment untill 1936 when I saw a Poster of Kitchener to say your Country needs join the Army and see the World so this appealed to me as I was working for a Pound a week and the Army was offering fourteen shillings a week full board so off I went to Belfast on a push Bike I had bought for five shillings. and set off for Belfast, When I reached Glengormilly I stored my bike at the cost of one old penny and travelled the rest of the Way to the Recruiting Office by tram, but I was about the middle of the City I came accross rioting and soldiers on the street but I was escorted to Alfred Street where the Recruiting Office was in 1935 where I was met by a Busley Sergeant Major of the Guards Regiment who took my height and an Education Exams. plus a Medical etc, but I was sent home again as I was under age.

I went back again in September 20th 1936 I went to work as usual in the morning of the Twentieth and came home as usal for dinner But When I got my father and rest of my family out of the way I said to my mother I was going away to the Army although I was still under age and this time I succeeded and left home for Belfast and met a pal there who was also joining up I was going to join the Scotch Greys as they were a Horse Regiment at this time, but as there was no recruiting

4

for that Regiment, I was asked about the Irish Guards
so I accepted and passed with flying colours

My Pal and I who was about ten years older than me
received our Bottom money a days pay and the Kings
Shilling when we signed the dotted line

We went to the Cinema to pass the time and as I
had an uncle living in Belfast we paid them a visit
until it was time make our way to the boat

In the meantime my father and my sister had
arrived at my uncle's place to try and persuade me
to change my mind but my mind was made up
and I and my pal arrived at the Guards Training
Depot on the 22nd September 1936 at app. 1 p.m. just
as a parade was about to start

When we had booked in to the Guard Room and
awaited our escort we heard this temendous voice
which nearly rocked the Guardroom, and when our escort
arrived to take us to our destination he went so fast
accross the Parade ground we we left trailing a long
way behind so I shouted at our escort to take his
time he replied not me mate I would be booked
and get punished for being idle

When we reached our destination when was the
receiving Room we were met by a train Soldier by the
name of Scott to took us in hand and gave us
a few lessons etc. in this room was a mixture of
Grenadiers Welsh, Scotch & Irish Recruits and this train
soldier's job was to show us how to make our bed up
in the morning for Room Inspection and general he seemed
a pleasant chap who came from Belfast and had quite
a bit of Service in.

When we were awoke by the Duty drummer the next

4

morning at six o'clock and when the last notes of Reveille were sounded on his Bugle our feet had to be on the floor, and start making up our beds etc. and if it wasn't to his liking we had to make it up until it was perfect

After a short stay at the receiving room we were transferred to the Training Company Number Five where we we met by the Company Sgt Major Murphy who put us at ease until we were sent round to the Army Doctor who took us to the football field after being kitted out in shorts vest and running shoes and to start running round the football field until you either dropped with exaustion or was still running you we accepted as fit.

We were then taken into a Room where we were asked questions regarding when we joined and what it took to be a soldier, and some of them put their hands and said "Sir" I know what it takes "brains" Sir and the doctor replied not in your nelly it takes guts and any one here who hasn't got that get on your way.

We were then issued with our kits of Clothing Boots etc and handed a U Blanket and spread it on the ground at the store room where the storeman started to chuck all kinds of Clothing etc into the blanket and sent at the double to another storeroom where all your kit was stencilled showing your Army Number etc. in case any items got purched.

When our Numbers reached twenty or Twenty Four we were formed into a Squad and our Soldiering days had begin.

We had a shinning parade each evening from 4 30 PM to 5 30 PM when all equipment for parade the next

5

morning had to be properly cleaned and inspected by your Instructor, when it passed him the squad had to assemble outside the block in Gym kit order and proceed to the Baths, where everyone had to have a cold shower winter or summer, that once we were marched back to our Barrack Room, and made stand on the end of the bed and show feet & hands clean to the Instructor that finished we were paraded for supper.

and then more skinning of boots etc you were expected to be able to shave by the shine on the toe of your boots. Discipline was very strict and anyone who would not accept the discipline were in deep trouble.

Everything was done by Numbers, and we were only allowed out of Depot one night a week, and had to be inspected by the Guard Commander, and passed by him.

We were very fit when we left the Depot after a gruelling eighteen weeks of intensive train, they either make or break you in the Guards Depot in my time of service.

While I was at the Training Depot I entered most of the sports, and became a good Cross Country Runner, came in third in the combined Services in 1936 at Cranwell and landed up in Medical Centre that night with the Flu.

I was also very good in the Gym with the Horse Wall Bars, Rope Climbing, Matt, Cross Bar, good all round. Our Gym Instructor Sergeant Shirlow recommended a Recruit H. Crossen & myself as good material.

I was also a first Class shot with the Rifle a became a Marksman. with the Rifle, Lewis Gun, and later on in years with the Bren Gun.

We finished our Recruit Training in December 1936 as passed out as a good Squad.

6

Went on Leave in January 1937 for Twenty one days known as Embarcation Leave, and then embarked on the Troopship at Southampton for Egypt and joined the Battalion in the Sahara Desert in March 1937 on Manouvers and got klimatized to the heat which was severe, but we enjoyed every moment of it. We were put on Active Service fighting in the middle 1937 because of Unrest in the Capital City of Cairo and this lasted for a long time if we walked out town we must be in threes never alone and carry a Dog Stick in case we got attacked and many a time the situation was tence and we kept clear of the troubled areas, but most of time we were on Manouvers in the Desert, and Trooping the Colour practise back in Barracks and getting reddy for the big day. We did not care too much for that practice as it was so hot and we had Revallie about three O'Clock in the morning and after breakfast we went on parade which lasted until 8 am or 9 am as it was too warm to continue some of the men were fainting on parade and dropping their Rifle which was an offence in my Days and were punished on return by Confining you to Barracks for seven days or more plus extra parades in full marching order and that was no joke in the heat of the day

I remember one Sunday Morning when I was lined up on parade for inspection before marching to Church the Sergant in Waiting began to inspect the men and when he came to a chap beside me and asked him when he shaved last and was put on a charge this chap had a accident on his chin before joining the Army and it bore a scare I was also charged for not shaving and I had nothing

7

to shave as I was only seventeen years of age then, but
I had to show myself shaved on an extra parade.
We were on the Ranges early one morning shortly
after Dawn for practice to see if any of us could make
the shooting team and I was picked for the team
and my room-mate was on the Butts signalling each
hit when he needed to use the toilet for water-works
purpose and one of the other Guardsmen saw my mate
urinating at the butts and reported him to the Officer in
charge who in turn put my mate on a charge to attend
Company Orders at a certain time which my mate died
and the Officer trying my mate for the Offence and
if it was me I would have done the same myself
Seven Days confined to camp plus four extra parades
fallout.
One morning when we came from the Ranges and were
about to clean I Rifles, the duty bugler sounded the Battalian
fall in and we were all briefed at the trouble in Palestine and
we were needed to reinforce the troops there, so we packed out
kit and moved out of our camp and back to Kasr-el-nil Barracks
in Cairo, and be ready to move out to Palestine by road
transport trough the Sahara Desert and cross into Palestine
at a place call Moasker, but on way through the desert we had
sand storms and the roads were no more than tracks marking
the road were tin barrels which were covered over with sand
so we had to use our own inititise and sometimes we went off
the track and ended up in sand dunes, and had quite a
job getting back onto the right track again
After hours of travelling we came to our destination at
Moasker, and after a brew up and Bullybeef sandwitches
we embarked on the Barrage and cross the Canal into
Palestine where we boarded the train which had woodenseats

8

which was very uncomfortable and you could either sit inside or outside as there were seats outside the carraige and some inside so many of us choose to sit outside to get a better view of the country side, but there was a chance of getting ambushed by terrorists so we allways had to be ready for action if the time came, but thank God we travelled hundred of miles with no mishaps until we arrived at Tulkarm Railway Station where we had another brew-up and another train drew up travelling in the opposite direction, which happened to be a hospital train taking the wounded to hospital. I opened the window of my apartment and spoke to one of the wounded men who enquired what regiment we were and I said the Irish Guards and he said if I knew of anyone with the name Quigley on board and I said did he know anyone of that name so after a while I found out he was a neighbour of mine and had joined the Ulster Rifles in 1930 so I said its a small world.

After our brief stop we were off again on our way to Nablus Fort where we arrived shattered, and started to settle in our new surroundings in tents between two mountains and a couple of days later when we got settled in, and we were having a quiet drink in the Naffi tent at 8·30PM. when our duty Bugler turned the Last Post into the alarm, and then there was panic stations to get our rifles etc, as they were chained up in the tent. This attack lasted for some time and our Commanding Officer was crawling around the lines shouting cease fire but nobody heard until they run out of ammo.

We used to go to the Cinema at night which was out in the open and the film was shown on a whitewashed wall, we sat there with our rifles between our legs in case being attacked by the Arabs

45

9

Our job was to keep the peace between the two factions Arab and Jews and to disarm them to the best of our ability. We were there for a few months, and at the end of November we were ordered by the War Office to proceed to Haifa and embark on a troopship and to return to Cairo in Egypt, where we began to pack up and return to England.

We arrived back in England on the 17th December 1938 and moved into the Tower of London Barracks.

Were sent on a month disembarkation leave and then resumed Public Duties until March 1939 when we moved to Pirbright Camp to fire a course with the Bren Gun and retrain the reservists who were called up for six weeks training.

We moved to Wellington Barracks to resume Public Duties etc in July when the 2nd Bn. was reformed I joined them and September we moved to Windsor and the Reservists were called up as War was declared on Germany, and after rigorous training to get the men fit for War.

We moved back to Wellington Barracks again and were joined by the 1st Battalion once more.

We were put on Red Alert and had to patrol the streets of London at night in case of riotting or looting of shops etc.

In 1940 the 1st Bn. moved out of Wellington Barracks and 2nd Bn. moved out shortly after for further field training to Dean Common Camberley undr Canvas where we trained until May 1940 when we were ordered to pack up and we were off to the Hook of Holland as it was about to fall to the German Army Our task completed in Holland we returned to England and once more to Dean Common Camberley

10

where we were rekitted out again as most of our Equipment was lost in Holland.

We returned to Dean Common Camberley and I missed the Roll Call and when I reported to my Company Commander and Company Sergem Major and saw what was left of my equipment where it was shot to pieces by the german planes as they straffed our Head Quarters after dropping their bombs close to the American Hotel When my equipment was examined I found a piece of Schrapnel in my messtin which I

Handwritten notes were done in the months before Sam Quigley's passing.
Illness prevented him from completion.

Soldier's Service Book

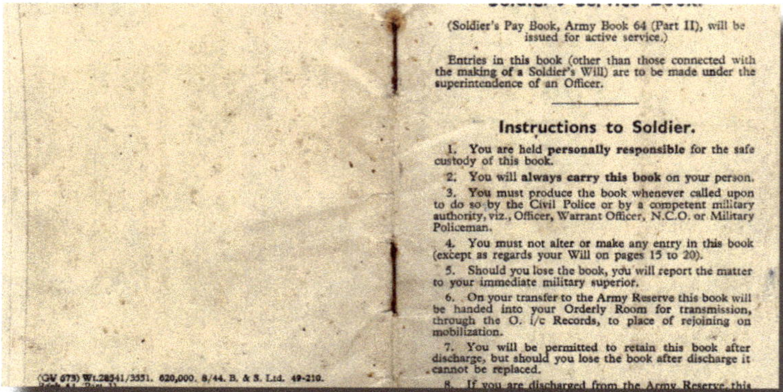

(GV 673) Wt.28541/3551. 620,000. 8/44. B. & S. Ltd. 49-210.

(Soldier's Pay Book, Army Book 64 (Part II), will be issued for active service.)

Entries in this book (other than those connected with the making of a Soldier's Will) are to be made under the superintendence of an Officer.

Instructions to Soldier.

1. You are held **personally responsible** for the safe custody of this book.
2. You will **always carry this book** on your person.
3. You must produce the book whenever called upon to do so by the Civil Police or by a competent military authority, viz., Officer, Warrant Officer, N.C.O. or Military Policeman.
4. You must not alter or make any entry in this book (except as regards your Will on pages 15 to 20).
5. Should you lose the book, you will report the matter to your immediate military superior.
6. On your transfer to the Army Reserve this book will be handed into your Orderly Room for transmission, through the O. i/c Records, to place of rejoining on mobilization.
7. You will be permitted to retain this book after discharge, but should you lose the book after discharge it cannot be replaced.
8. If you are discharged from the Army Reserve this

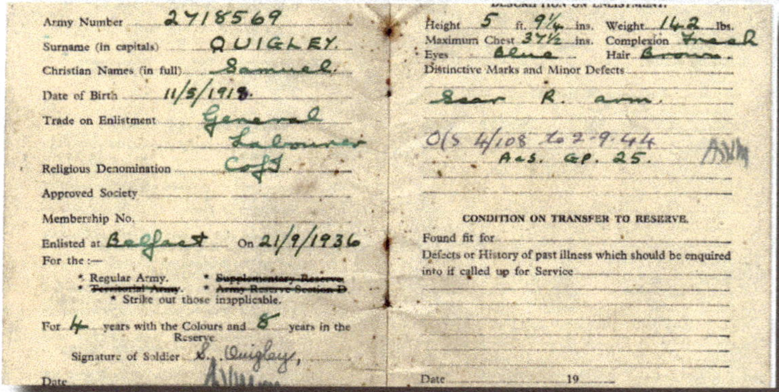

Army Number 2718569
Surname (in capitals) QUIGLEY.
Christian Names (in full) Samuel.
Date of Birth 11/5/1918.
Trade on Enlistment General Labourer
Religious Denomination C of I.
Approved Society
Membership No.
Enlisted at Belfast On 21/9/1936
For the :—
* Regular Army. * ~~Supplementary Reserve~~
* ~~Territorial Army~~. * ~~Army Reserve Section D~~
* Strike out those inapplicable.
For 4 years with the Colours and 8 years in the Reserve.
Signature of Soldier S. Quigley,
Date

Height 5 ft. 9¼ ins. Weight 142 lbs.
Maximum Chest 37½ ins. Complexion Fresh
Eyes Blue Hair Brown.
Distinctive Marks and Minor Defects
Scar R. arm.
O/S 4/108 to 2-9-44
A.&S. GP. 25.

CONDITION ON TRANSFER TO RESERVE.

Found fit for
Defects or History of past illness which should be enquired into if called up for Service

Date 19

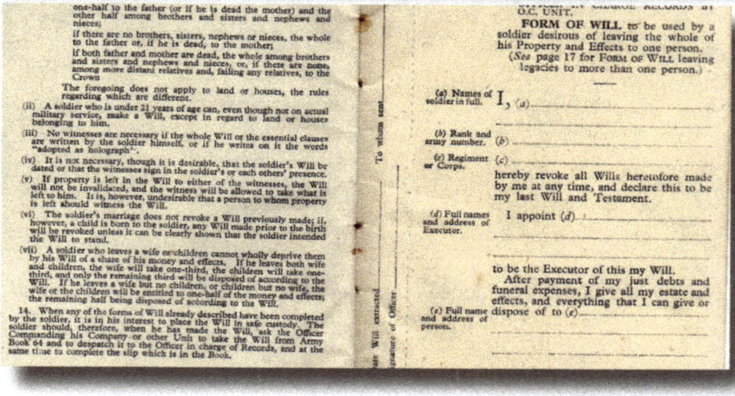

one-half to the father (or if he is dead the mother) and the other half among brothers and sisters and nephews and nieces;

if there are no brothers, sisters, nephews or nieces, the whole to the father or, if he is dead, to the mother;

if both father and mother are dead, the whole among brothers and sisters and nephews and nieces, or, if there are none, among more distant relatives and, failing any relatives, to the Crown

The foregoing does not apply to land or houses, the rules regarding which are different.

(ii) A soldier who is under 21 years of age can, even though not on actual military service, make a Will, except in regard to land or houses belonging to him.

(iii) No witnesses are necessary if the whole Will or the essential clauses are written by the soldier himself, or if he writes on it the words "adopted as holograph".

(iv) It is not necessary, though it is desirable, that the soldier's Will be dated or that the witnesses sign in the soldier's or each others' presence.

(v) If property is left in the Will to either of the witnesses, the Will will not be invalidated, and the witness will be allowed to take what is left to him. It is, however, undesirable that a person to whom property is left should witness the Will.

(vi) The soldier's marriage does not revoke a Will previously made; if, however, a child is born to the soldier, any Will made prior to the birth will be revoked unless it can be clearly shown that the soldier intended the Will to stand.

(vii) A soldier who leaves a wife or children cannot wholly deprive them by his Will of a share of his money and effects. If he leaves both wife and children, the wife will take one-third, the children will take one-third, and only the remaining third will be disposed of according to the Will. If he leaves a wife but no children, or children but no wife, the wife or the children will be entitled to one-half of the money and effects; the remaining half being disposed of according to the Will.

14. When any of the forms of Will already described have been completed by the soldier, it is in his interest to place the Will in safe custody. The soldier should, therefore, when he has made the Will, ask the Officer Commanding his Company or other Unit to take the Will from Army Book 64 and to despatch it to the Officer in charge of Records, and at the same time to complete the slip which is in the Book.

Date Will extracted
To whom sent
Signature of Officer

O.C. UNIT.

FORM OF WILL to be used by a soldier desirous of leaving the whole of his Property and Effects to one person.
(*See* page 17 for FORM OF WILL leaving legacies to more than one person.)

(*a*) Names of soldier in full. I, (*a*)
(*b*) Rank and army number. (*b*)
(*c*) Regiment or Corps. (*c*)
hereby revoke all Wills heretofore made by me at any time, and declare this to be my last Will and Testament.
(*d*) Full names and address of Executor. I appoint (*d*)
to be the Executor of this my Will.
After payment of my just debts and funeral expenses, I give all my estate and effects, and everything that I can give or dispose of to (*e*)
(*e*) Full name and address of person.

_____, as and
for his last Will, in the presence of us,
present at the same time, who, in his
presence, at his request, and in the presence
of each other, have hereunto subscribed
our names as Witnesses.*

(i) Signature (i) _____
of 1st Witness.

(j) Address or (j) _____
rank, regimental
No. and Unit.

(k) Signature (k) _____
of 2nd Witness.

(l) Address or (l) _____
rank, regimental
No. and Unit.   * N.B.—The Witnesses must *NOT* be
persons intended to benefit under the Will,
or husbands or wives of such persons.

another or others.

(*See* page 15 for FORM OF
everything to one person

(a) Names of   I, (a) _____
soldier in full.

(b) Rank and (b) _____
army number.

(c) Regiment (c) _____
or Corps.
hereby revoke all Wills here
by me at any time, and decla
my last Will and Testament.

(d) Full name   I appoint (d) _____
and address of
Executor.

to be the Executor of this m
After payment of my just
(e) Full name Funeral Expenses I give to (e
and address of
person.

(f) State the (f) _____
particular
articles or
money intended and I give to (e) _____
to be given.

(f) _____

(e) _____

(g) Date.   Signed this (g) _____ day of _____ 19__

(h) Signature (h) _____
of soldier.

(i) Insert full   Signed and acknowledged by the said (i)
name of soldier
making the Will.
_____, as and
for his last Will, in the presence of us,
present at the same time, who, in his
presence, at his request, and in the presence
of each other, have hereunto subscribed
our names as Witnesses.*

(j) Signature (j) _____
of 1st Witness.

(k) Address (k) _____
or rank, regi-
mental No. and
Unit.

(l) Signature (l) _____
of 2nd Witness.

(m) Address (m) _____
or rank, regi-
mental No. and
Unit.   * N.B.—The Witnesses must NOT be
persons intended to benefit under the Will,
or husbands or wives of such persons.

SHORT FORM OF WILL.
(Write Will on next page.)

If a soldier in actual military service wishes to make a short Will,
he may do so on the next page. It must be entirely in his own
handwriting, and must be signed by him and dated. The full
names and addresses of the persons whom he desires to benefit, and
the sum of money or the articles of property which he desires to
leave to them, must be clearly stated. The mere entry of the
name of an intended legatee on the next page without any
mention of what the legatee is to receive is of no legal
value.

The following is a specimen of a Will leaving all to one person :—

In the event of my death I give the whole of my property and
effects to my mother, Mrs. Mary Bull, 999, High Street, Aldershot.
(*Signature*) GEORGE BULL,
Fusilier, No. 1973, Royal Fusrs.
Date 5th August, 1914.

The following is a specimen of a Will leaving legacies to more
than one person :—

In the event of my death I give £10 to my friend, Miss Rose
Smith, of No. 1, High Street, London, and I give £5 to my
sister, Miss Maud Bull, 999, High Street, Aldershot, and I give
the remaining part of my property to my mother, Mrs. Mary
Bull, 999 High Street, Aldershot.
(*Signature*) GEORGE BULL,
Fusilier, No. 1973, Royal Fusrs.
Date 5th August, 1914.

Soldiers are, however, recommended to make a formal Will before
embarkation on A.F.B. 2089, or one of the forms of formal Will
provided on pp. 15 and p. 17, and to hand it to their Commanding
Officer for transmission to the Record Office for safe custody.

This Will page must NOT be used until you have been
placed in actual Military Service.

WILL.

(For use if the soldier has not already made a Will or wishes to
alter one already made. See instructions on previous page.)
ON COMPLETION TO BE DESPATCHED TO OFFICER IN
CHARGE RECORDS BY O.C. UNIT.

Signature _____

Rank and Regiment _____

Army Number _____

Date _____

RECORD OF SPECIALIST EMPLOYMENT WHILST SERVING.*

Period.		Nature of Employment.	Remarks and In of Officer.
From	To		
		LEAVE	FREE WARRANT
-25-8-45		COMPASSIONATE	YES
5-2-9-45		48 hrs V.J.	No.

NEXT OF KIN.

No change will be made in this page unless it is notified to an Officer who will
initial the new entry and ensure that it is reported in Part II/III Orders.
NOTE.—No entry in this page has any legal effect as a Will (see pages 12 to

Name and latest known Address in full.	Date of Entry.	Initial Offic
Section 1. Enter here the Name and Address of the person whom you wish to be notified if anything should happen to you. You are not compelled to nominate your wife if you are married, but if her name is not given there may be delay before she receives the news. Name *Sofia Quigley* Relationship (if any) *wife* Address *72, Selandbourne,* *Muckamore, Co. Antrim*	24/7/45	M
New Address		
New Address		
Section 2. To be completed only if the person entered above is changed. Name Relationship (if any) Address		
New Address		
New Address		
Section 3. To be completed only if the person entered at Sections 1 and 2 is changed. Name Relationship (if any) Address		
New Address		

Soldier's Pay Book

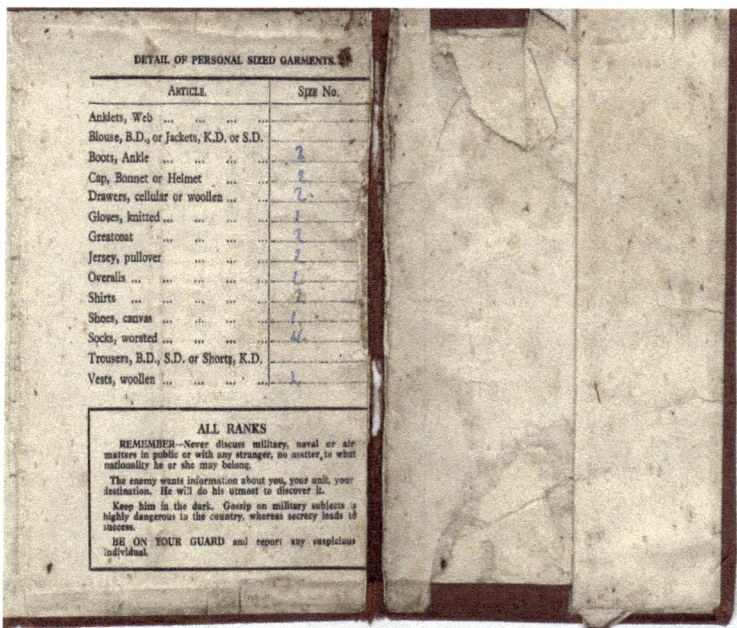

DETAIL OF PERSONAL SIZED GARMENTS.

Article.	Size No.
Anklets, Web	
Blouse, B.D., or Jackets, K.D. or S.D.	
Boots, Ankle	2
Cap, Bonnet or Helmet ...	2
Drawers, cellular or woollen ...	2
Gloves, knitted	1
Greatcoat	2
Jersey, pullover	2
Overalls	1
Shirts	2
Shoes, canvas	1
Socks, worsted	4
Trousers, B.D., S.D. or Shorts, K.D.	
Vests, woollen	1

ALL RANKS

REMEMBER—Never discuss military, naval or air matters in public or with any stranger, no matter to what nationality he or she may belong.

The enemy wants information about you, your unit, your destination. He will do his utmost to discover it.

Keep him in the dark. Gossip on military subjects is highly dangerous to the country, whereas secrecy leads to success.

BE ON YOUR GUARD and report any suspicious individual.

Imperial Service Medal

. 49801

9443

SECOND SUPPLEMENT TO

The London Gazette

of Monday, 9th July 1984

Published by Authority

Registered as a Newspaper

TUESDAY, 10TH JULY 1984

CENTRAL CHANCERY OF
THE ORDERS OF KNIGHTHOOD

St. James's Palace, London S.W.1.

10th July, 1984

he QUEEN has been graciously pleased to award
ie Imperial Service Medal to the following officers
n their retirement.

Ministry of Agriculture, Fisheries and Food

ʻOBITT, Alexander Charles, Chief Photoprinter.

Ministry of Defence

ᴧCTON, Thomas Oliver, Professional and Technology Officer III.
ᴧDAMS, Leslie William, Process and General Sup-
ervisory C.
ᴧDAMS, Lewis Frederick, Caulker/Riveter/Burner/
Driller.
ᴧLLEN, Reginald Daniel, Motor Transport Driver.
ᴃAILEY, David Gordon George, Professional and
Technology Officer III.
ᴃAKER, Sidney Roy, Joiner.
ᴃATES, David Thomas, Craftsman.
ᴃAXTER, William James, Government Telephonist.
ᴃEATTIE, Arthur William, Driver.
ᴃEATTIE, Clarence Richard James, Experimental
Worker III.
ᴃLACKBURN, Herbert, Setter A.
ᴃLAINEY, John Harvey, Electrician II.
ᴃRADLEY, Frank, Mechanical Transport Driver.
ᴄOOK, David Walter, Professional and Technology
Officer III.

COOK, Frederick Arthur, Driver.
CORCORAN, Edward, Craftsman.
CREED, Donald, Fitter/Turner.
CURTIS, Ronald Arthur, Professional and Techɴ
logy Officer IV.
DAVISON, Ralph, Professional and Technolɐ
Officer III.
DOCHERTY, Robert, Chargehand Joiner.
DRISCOLL, Wilfred, Senior Storekeeper.
DUNNING, Herbert George, Professional and Te
nology Officer IV.
EDNEY, William Charles, Professional and Tech
logy Officer IV.
ELLESTON, Arthur Henry, Photoprinter I.
FAIR, Ronald Henry, Machinist.
FAIRWAY, Douglas, Shipwright.
FENN, Eric Arthur, Storekeeper.
FIRKINS, George John, Professional and Technol
Officer IV.
FORBES, Alexander Samuel, Professional and Tɛ
nology Officer III.
GARD, Alan William, Professional and Technol
Officer IV.
GOLDIE, James Anderson, BEM, Stores Offi
Grade C.
GOODRICK, Mrs. May Dorothy, Chief Photoprir
GOULDING, Victor John, Messenger.
GREAGG, Alan Victor, Chargehand.
HEDGECOCK, Mrs. Sarah, Stores Officer Grade D.
HOLT, Kenneth George, Process and General Su
visory E.
HOPPER, Robert Henry, Industrial Technician.
JEFF, Robert, Welder.
JENKIN, Aubrey Freethy, Professional and Tec
logy Officer IV.

9444   SUPPLEMENT TO THE LONDON GAZETTE, 10TH JULY 1984

KITT, Terence London, Assistant Chief Photoprinter.
LEECH, Thurston Henry, Professional and Technology Officer III.
LODGE, Frank, Aircraft Fitter.
LUCOCK, Ernest, Storekeeper.
McDERMOTT, James Robert, Head Messenger.
MACDONALD, Thomas Hector, Professional and Technology Officer IV.
McKINLAY, Angus Currie, Fitter Mechanical.
MADGE, William Samuel Robert, Qualified Assistant Painter.
MORGAN, Sidney Thomas, Progressman Non Technical.
NEIL, Mrs. Jean McDonald, Cleaner Chargehand.
PHILLIPS, William Alan, Professional and Technology Officer IV.
PURDY, Thomas, Marine Services Officer IV.
QUIGLEY, Samuel Leading Armed Patrolman.
QUINNELL, John Peter, Professional and Technology Officer IV.
RIEKIE, Mrs. Grace Mary, Production Worker I Chargehand.
ROBERTS, Frederick, Setter Auto Single.
ROGERS, Miss Audrey May, Instrument Mechanic.
SIMPSON, James Reginald, Examiner II.
SKIRVING, William, Professional and Technology Officer IV.
SMITH, Thomas Andrew, Stores Officer Grade C.
STONE, Kenneth Arthur, Professional and Technology Officer IV.
STOWELL, Arthur James, Storeman I.
THIRWALL, William, Senior Storeman.
TINSON, Maurice Edgar, Radio Technician.
TUCKER, William Edward, Crane Driver.
TURNER, Stanton, Steward II.
TYTE, Miss Mary Eileen, Higher Grade Cartographic Draughtsman.
VERNAL, David McNair Walls, Professional and Technology Officer IV.
WALKER, Raymond Leslie, Stores Officer Grade C.
WASHINGTON, James, Production Worker I.
WEBB, Reginald William, Craftsman.
WEIR, Alexander, Examiner I.
WELLS, Leslie, Steward II.
WHITMORE, Alan, Professional and Technology Officer IV.
WILLIAMSON, James William, Skilled Labourer.

Department of the Environment

FLINT, Robert John, Chargehand Mason.
GOWLETT, Maurice Benjamin, Professional and Technology Officer III.
JOHNSON, Charles Wilfred, Driver III.
JONES, Reginald, Fitter Mechanic.
KING, Maurice George, Professional and Technology Officer III.

ORCHARD, Ernest George Albert, Professional and Technology Officer III.
TOMKINS, Frederick John, Craft Auxiliary Worker A.

Government Communications Headquarters

ADAM, Ernest Watt McAndrew, Station Radio Officer.
ADDISON, John, Radio Officer.
ASBURY, Edward Foster, Radio Officer.
BELTON, Raymond John, Station Radio Officer.
BICE, Albert Arthur, Station Radio Officer.
FAIRBAIRN, John Graham, Radio Officer.
HARDING, Kenneth John Dunstan, Radio Officer.
HUNTER, John, Station Radio Officer.
McCREEDY, Alex Richard, Station Radio Officer.
McLEAN, Thomas Stewart Fulton, Radio Officer.
PAXTON, Frederick George, Radio Officer.
PRICE, Arthur Sydney John, Radio Officer.
SMITH, Raymond Charles, Station Radio Officer.
TAIT, Edward, Station Radio Officer.

Home Office

BAILEY, George, Bricklayer, H.M. Prison, Sudbury.
BROWN, Frederick Cecil, Senior Storeman, Supply and Transport Store, Branston.
FLANIGAN, George Frederick, Senior Officer, H.M. Prison, Chelmsford.
FULCHER, Patrick John, Officer, H.M. Prison, Wandsworth.
HOWE, Peter, Senior Hospital Officer, H.M. Prison, Pentonville.
HOWSON, Dudley Thomas, Officer Instructor, H.M. Detention Centre, Aldington.
MEIN, Peter John, Senior Officer, H.M. Prison, Winchester.
POULTER, Albert Edmund, Senior Officer, H.M. Prison, Lewes.
SIBLEY, Arthur, Officer, H.M. Prison, Ford.
TUCK, John Orton, Chief Officer I, Inspectorate of Prisons, Queen Anne's Gate.

Ordnance Survey

BOOTH, James Albert, Professional and Technology Officer IV.
BROOKS, David Phillip, Surveyor Higher Grade.
ENDERBY, Millson, Surveyor Basic Grade.
FRIEL, Thomas Patrick, Surveyor Higher Grade.

Her Majesty's Stationery Office

EYRE, Mrs. Jean Winifred, Warehousewoman.
MARTIN, Dennis John, Bookseller.
STAWARSKI, Mrs. Elizabeth Catherine, Assistant Chief Photoprinter.
URSELL, Mrs. Margaret, Assistant Chief Photoprinter.

LONDON
Printed and published by HER MAJESTY'S STATIONERY OFFICE: 1984
Price £1·00 net

PRINTED IN ENGLAND

ISBN 0 11 659801 8
ISSN 0261-8575

R.U.C.
Certificate of Character

Certificate No. 760

ROYAL ULSTER CONSTABULARY.

FORM $\frac{37}{3}$

Certificate of Character.*

On discharge of No. 5845 (Rank) Constable
(Name) Samuel Quigley who joined
above-named Force on the 17th day of April, 1 94
and was discharged on the 8th day of May, 1 94
in consequence of (†) resignation

His general conduct during the period of his service was very good

DESCRIPTION ON DISCHARGE.

Age, 27 years. Height, 5 ft. 10½ ins.
Colour of Hair, Brown. Colour of Eyes, Blue.
Complexion, Fresh.
Special distinguishing } None.
Marks (if any) }

Parish and County where born Randalstown, Co. Antrim.
Single, Married, or Widower, Married.
R.U.C. Depot,
Given under my hand and seal at Enniskillen this 8th
day of May, 1 948.

Signature

Rank Commandant of ‡ R.U.C. Depot,
Enniskillen,
Co. Ferman

* This Certificate is given without alteration or erasure.
† Insert here the circumstances under which the discharge takes place.
‡ Insert name of County

1483-107035 W11414-HO805 2000 G10 Wm. S. & Sons, Ltd.

Sam's Photo Gallery

Sam Quigley

Sam Quigley

**Sam, when presented with the Imperial Service Medal
at Ballykinlar, Northern Ireland in 1984**

MY LIFE AS A GIRL IN WARTIME GERMANY

Sophia Freda Rohl

The 25th of December 1925 was the day that I was born in Friedrichfelde, West Germany.

I was the fifth child born to Elizabeth Rohl. Sadly, I never knew my father. He was in the Navy and whilst serving in India, died of a tropical disease three months before I was born. I never did get to know much about him, not even his name. I had three sisters and one brother: Anni, Mimi, Lotti and Adolph.

When I was about eighteen months old, my mother got remarried to Ronald Rohl, who was a relative of my father. I later had a younger half-sister and brother, Kate and Eric.

My stepfather owned a market garden, but because he was too lazy to work, all of us children had to do the work. I remember being put to work when I was about five years old. It was very hard work, and I had to work in the mornings before school and again when school finished. As a child, I felt terrible and never had any sort of childhood.

At about the age of eight, my stepfather went bankrupt. He then bought a pub, and with this, he inherited a lot of debt from the previous owners, although he did not know this at the time of buying it. I remember a man and a woman who were staying at the pub, they didn't have any children, and the man offered my stepfather enough money to pay off his debts and have some left over if he could have one of his children. My stepfather offered to sell me. I cried and cried at the thought of not seeing my brothers and sisters again, and on seeing how upset I was, the man and woman decided not to take me. I ended up being beaten by my stepfather with 'the cat.' I remember 'the cat' very well, a handle with nine leather thongs on it, and I was beaten with it many times.

My stepfather was not a good man. I always felt that he did not like me, and I believe this was because of my mother's family. He was always very hard on me. We all had to work hard, but I and my brother Adolph were the ones who always got beaten. If my stepfather did not have his drink or cigarettes, he took it out on us. That's probably why I never drank or smoked. I promised myself that if I ever got married and had children, they would never suffer the way that I did.

We lived at the pub for about nine months and then moved to a farm on the German/Polish border. I cannot remember the name of the exact place.

The routine remained the same, hard work for us children on the farm before and after school - still no childhood.

The farm was on the Polish side of the border, and we went to school on the German side, and because we had been living outside of Germany for more than five years, we lost our German nationality.

In September 1939, when I was almost fifteen years old, war broke out and in moved the German soldiers. They came to our farm and took all of our household possessions and farm animals, giving everything to the German people living in Germany. No one would believe that we were German. Our farm was taken over by the German soldiers and we had to leave our home, taking only what we could carry with us. I could only manage to carry some clothes. I didn't have anything special to take with me, no toys, nothing.

We were made to wear P tags to show that we were Polish.

What followed was a seven-mile walk to the nearest railway station, where we were hoarded onto cattle wagons with lots of other Polish families and taken to Brenz in East Germany. At the railway station in Brenz, we were met by local farmers who were waiting to take their pick of who they wanted to work on their farms.

My whole family were separated to go and work on different farms, with the exception of my younger brother, who was allowed to stay with my mother and stepfather. The only feelings that I remember about being separated from my family was that of relief at getting away from my stepfather. I was very sad at the prospect of possibly never seeing my brothers and sisters again.

I went to work at a farm in Brenz, and I'd been working there for about three months when I learnt that my sister Mimi was working in the same village. I went to visit her, and she told me where the rest of the family was.

Working on the farm was hard, but I was well-fed, and at least I was away from the wicked hands of my stepfather and, of course, 'the cat.'

I got paid 25 Deutsche Marks per month, and all of this I had to hand over to my stepfather.

I gave my money to Mimi, who then went to our older sister Anni and gave both our wages to her, who then handed it over to 'him'. I couldn't spend the money myself because being classed as Polish, the Germans wouldn't sell anything to us.

During the three years that I spent working in Brenz, my mother's family were fighting to get us our German Nationality back and they finally won. We were allowed to take the P tags off and were no longer classed as Polish. By this time and with the help of all the families wages, my stepfather had saved enough money to buy a farm in Helburg.

My mother, stepfather and younger brother moved to the farm in Helburg. The rest of us remained on the farms that we were working on.

Sometime later, I got an infection in my finger which developed into gangrene, and I could no longer work on the farm. I then went 'home' to Helburg, and what an appropriate name, back to hell with my stepfather. He didn't care what had happened to my finger and I had to work for him on his farm. It was 1943, and I was almost eighteen years old now.

My other brother and sisters remained working on the different farms and occasionally they came to visit, but we never lived as a family again. Adolph was called up to join the army.

I had a friend Toni, who came to work on our farm and we got on very well together, becoming close friends.

Other farm workers consisted of British Prisoners of War who were held at a prison in Wolfshagen and every day the German prison guards would bring about ten prisoners to the farm.

It was about November 1944 when I first saw this particular prisoner. He didn't have much hair and looked older than the rest, but for me it was love at first sight. I found out that his name was Sam and he was a friend of a prisoner who I know as Fyfer. Fyfer's real name was Tom Pyper and he and Toni became a couple.

When I got to know Sam, who spoke very good German, I told him about my horrible life with my stepfather and how badly he always treated me. Sam said, "I'll take you home to Ireland with me." I didn't believe him.

Sam and I started to see each other, but this was no easy task. I had to sneak out of the house at night, and Sam would break out of the prison camp. We would try to meet up about twice a week. If my stepfather had found out what I was doing, I dread to think what my punishment would have been.

I remember one night being in bed asleep when I was awakened by my hair being pulled.

It was Sam outside, and he had got a twig and twisted it into my hair to awaken me.

On another night in either March or April 1945, I sneaked out as usual to meet Sam, but British planes had been dropping bombs, and unbeknown to me, Sam couldn't get out of the prison camp. I went home and sneaked back into bed. I wasn't in bed long when my mother came and said that my stepfather wanted me. He asked me where I had been, and I had to lie. I told him that I had been outside to the toilet. I then got beaten with 'the cat'. He kept asking where I had been, and I kept saying that I was at the toilet, every time I answered him, he hit me. He said that he had been outside and didn't see me at the toilet. He didn't stop beating me until I said that I had been to the toilet by the dung heap.

I had huge cuts on my arm from the leather thongs.

The next day I had to go to the nearby village of Pulitz for bread. My step father told me to wear a cardigan to cover the marks on my arms but I took the cardigan off when I was out of his sight and when the baker asked what had happened, I told him. He said that my stepfather should have been locked up for doing such a thing.

In April 1945, the prisoners were to be moved from Wolfshagen and on the night before being moved, Sam and Tom escaped from the prison camp and hid in a shed about a quarter of a mile away from the farm. Toni and I would take food to them every night.

They stayed in hiding until about the 1st May 1945 when the Russian soldiers arrived.

On the 2nd May 1945, my stepfather was on the farm killing a bullock for the Polish workers, and I was standing watching with everyone else, but I was told to get inside and peel the potatoes for dinner. A Russian soldier followed me inside, and then my mother and stepfather came in. The Russian threw them out the door and trying to lock the door behind them. The door lock worked in the reverse way to normal, and he was having trouble locking the door. I sensed that he intended to attack me, so while he was preoccupied with the door lock, I jumped out of the window and ran for my life.

I ran across the farm yard, and I heard a gun shot as I was going through the door of the cow shed. I felt the bullet whistle through my hair. I laid myself down between two calves and stayed very still. The Russian soldier came looking for me, but thankfully he didn't find me.

When I was running away, I remember a girl in the farm yard who was clapping and laughing at what was happening to me. She wasn't as lucky as I was, and from what I know was at the mercy of several Russian soldiers. I found out the next day that the Russian soldier who had shot at me had raped other local girls, one of whom was so disturbed by what had happened to her that she slit her wrists and died.

Following these incidents, a Russian soldier of a more senior rank came visiting different homes in the area asking if any of his men had attacked any young girls. He was told about what happened, and I believe this soldier was later shot for what he had done.

I am glad I decided to jump out the window when I did.

Sam and Tom were more or less free to come and go as they pleased, and my stepfather now knew of my relationship with Sam, so I no longer had to sneak out of the house to see him.

My stepfather had not 'softened'; he had ulterior motives and thought that if he allowed me to see Sam; he would have us both working for him on the farm...little did he know.

On 4th May 1945, I was at home in the cellar; it was about half past ten at night, and my stepfather came and started shouting and calling me a bitch for not putting the cats out.

He twisted both my ears so hard that I honestly thought that he had ripped them off. I gathered up the cats, one under each arm and went to go through the door that my stepfather had opened and there, standing in the yard, were Sam, Tom and Toni.

I dropped the cats and ran and ran. That's the last time that I saw my stepfather, and at the time, all I felt was sheer relief at getting away from him, hopefully for good.

Sam and Tom had stolen a wagon and had it filled with provisions for the four of us and the horses. One of the horses just happened to belong to my stepfather and was the horse that he rode all the time, but now it was helping us to escape.

We travelled for eight days, arriving in Luneburg on 12th May 1945. This is when we found out that the war was over. We were given food and clothes and arrangements made for us to fly to Belgium and then on to London.

Once in London, Toni and I were taken to an ATS camp, and Tom and Sam had to return to their army barracks.

Sam and Tom had arranged a time to come back and collect us but they were late, and we were moved to another transit camp just outside London.

It was quite clear that if we 'not claimed' within four days, then the authorities would send us back to where we had come from. Our 'knights in shining armour' did find us and we made our way by train to Stranraer and then by boat to Larne, arriving in Ireland on the 21st May 1945. Sam certainly meant what he told me all those months before - that he would take me home to Ireland with him.

We arrived in Sam's village of Muckamore, Co. Antrim where

I was introduced to his family.

We were married on the 22nd of June 1945, but life was not plain sailing. Things were difficult as I could not speak very much English, and Sam's family could not speak German.

Sam had to return to his army barracks, and I stayed in Muckamore until September, when I went to England to be nearer Sam. I lived in a house in Reading, and Sam was in the army camp in Reading, so at least I could see him more often. I returned to Muckamore in December and Sam was de-mobbed in February 1946.

By this time, I was heavily pregnant and on the 25th March 1946, our first child Terry was born.

Sam joined the Royal Ulster Constabulary in April 1946, the same month that my stepfather died, but to be honest, I did not shed any tears when I heard the news.

Life got a little easier with the more English that I learnt, but I would never say that it was easy in the early days. We had more children; Jean arrived on the 17th September 1947, Edith on the 4th February 1950, Samuel on the 2nd May 1952 and Eric on the 28th October 1953. I kept in touch with my mother and my sisters, but I learnt that my stepfather never read any of my letters - he said that I went with the enemy. My mother came to Ireland for a holiday in 1957.

In September 1959, we moved to the small hamlet of Claragh in Co. Down, and I was pregnant again. With Eric being seven, I thought I had finished with babies, but on the 1st March 1960, Pamela was born and it started all over again.

Sam was now working as a Security Patrolman/Dog Handler at the army camp in Ballykinler.

I continued to stay in touch with my family in Germany, but I was never sure if my letters were reaching my sisters in East Germany.

My mother passed away in 1964, within a short space of time

of Sam's mother passing away.

I made my first trip back to Dortmund, West Germany in July 1967 to visit my mother's sister, Tante Mimi, and we spent several happy holidays with her over the years.

One by one, all of the children left home, with Pamela being the last to get married in June 1979. She moved to live in Germany, where her husband Martin was posted with the British Army.

In July 1980, Sam and I travelled to Buckeburg, Germany, to visit Pamela and Martin.

Arrangements had been made for my sister Mimi to travel from her home in East Germany to stay with us. The day finally arrived and we went to meet Mimi at the train station and although it had been forty years since I last saw her, I recognised her the minute she stepped off the train. We spent a lovely two weeks together catching up on each other's lives, and we had a great time - in some ways and with some of the things we did, it was like being two young girls again. One instance that I remember was the day that we visited a park and we were all playing on the children's slide - when Mimi came down, she forgot to put her feet down and she plopped straight on to the ground.

We all couldn't stop laughing, but poor Mimi had in fact, hurt herself. That is something that we never got to do as young sisters in East Germany, so we were trying to make up for those lost years. There was never any time for playing and enjoying ourselves - it was always work, work and more work.

Sadly, the two weeks came to an end all too quickly, and Mimi returned to East Germany, but we vowed that we would see each other again.

We stayed in touch, and when the Berlin wall came down, Mimi travelled with her son Ottmar to Northern Ireland for a holiday and that was the beginning of many happy and memorable trips made between us over the years. Sam and I travelled to Germany on many occasions to visit my family, and they, in return visited us in Ireland.

Sadly Sam took ill in 1995, and it was during a holiday in Germany to celebrate our 50th wedding anniversary that Sam was taken into hospital. Our stay was longer than planned because Sam was too ill to travel, but after several weeks he gained enough strength, and we were able to go home.

Sam's health deteriorated over the next two months, and he lost his battle against leukaemia and passed away on Sunday, 12th November 1995, which happened to be Remembrance Sunday.

My life goes on in Claragh, but I greatly miss my lifelong companion.

Freda's Documentation

Birth Certificate

E 1

Geburtsurkunde

(Standesamt Voerde (Niederrhein) Nr. 263/1925)

Frieda Margareta R ö h l

ist am 21. Dezember 1925

in Friedrichsfeld (Niederrhein) geboren.

Vater: Landwirt Reinhold Adolf Röhl,

wohnhaft in Friedrichsfeld (Niederrhein).

Änderungen der

Voerde (Niederrhein) . Mai 19 51.

STANDESBEAMTE

tretung:

A 51
Geburtsurkunde (eheliche Geburt)
Verlag für Standesamtswesen GmbH., burg — EK 172/150509 · 33 | A 51

Residential Permit

R.P. No. 59142

NORTHERN IRELAND
RESIDENCE PERMIT CARD.

CAUTION.

Care should be taken of this document. It should not be allowed to pass into the possession of an unauthorised person. If lost or destroyed the fact and circumstances should be reported immediately to the R.U.C.

Residential Permit

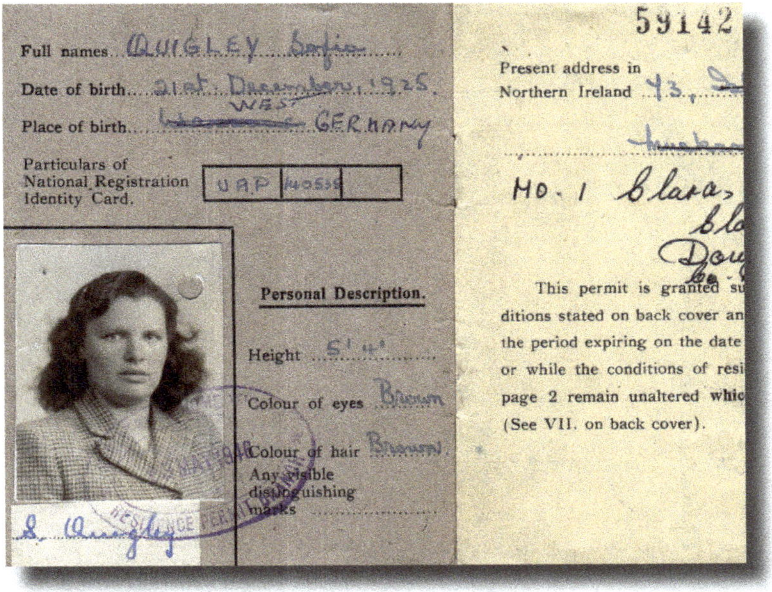

59142

Full names QUIGLEY Sofia

Date of birth 21st. December, 1925.

Place of birth ~~......~~ WEST GERMANY

Particulars of National Registration Identity Card. | UAP | 140535 | |

Personal Description.

Height 5' 4"

Colour of eyes Brown

Colour of hair Brown

Any visible distinguishing marks

S. Quigley

RESIDENCE PERMIT BRANCH

Present address in Northern Ireland 43, ...

No. 1 Clara, ...

This permit is granted su... ditions stated on back cover an... the period expiring on the date... or while the conditions of resi... page 2 remain unaltered whic... (See VII. on back cover).

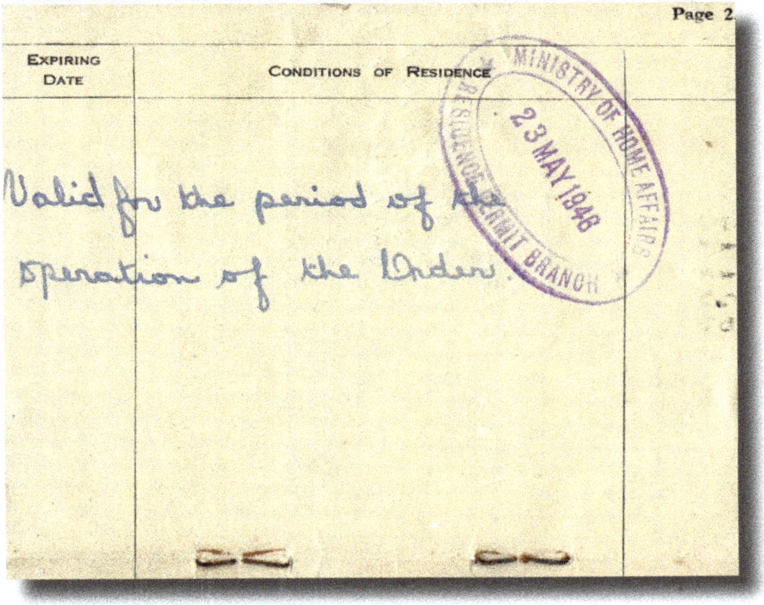

Page 2

Expiring Date	Conditions of Residence	
	Valid for the period of the operation of the Order.	

MINISTRY OF HOME AFFAIRS
23 MAY 1948
RESIDENCE PERMIT BRANCH

Northern Ireland Residence Permit.

I. Under Regulation 18 (2AA) of the Defence Regulations as applied by the Residence in Northern Ireland (Restriction) Order, 1942, all British subjects over the age of fourteen, except persons in the Service of the Crown, who were not on the first day of January, 1940, resident in Northern Ireland must, after the date (1st January, 1943) when the Order comes into force, hold a Residence Permit issued by the Ministry of Home Affairs (N.I.) if they reside in Northern Ireland for a continuous period of not less than six weeks.

II. Application for a Residence Permit (or renewal thereof) should be made on Form R.P. (or R.P.I.) to be obtained from any R.U.C. Station, or from the Ministry of Home Affairs, Residence Permit Branch, Belfast.

III. Applicants must furnish a recent photograph, in duplicate, taken full face without a hat and measuring not more than 3″ x 2″ or less than 3″ x 1½″.

IV. The fee for the issue or replacement of a Residence Permit is 2/6d. and for a renewal 1/6d.

V.   When completed, the application form must be lodged by the applicant at the R.U.C. Station of the district where he resides.

VI.   Documentary evidence in support of statements may be required.

VII.   Permits will be valid for a period of six months, or for the duration of the employment or other special reason for residence, whichever is the less.

VIII.   Applications for renewal of permits should be made if possible ten days before the date of expiry to the appropriate R.U.C. Station.

IX.   If a permit holder changes his address the permit must be produced without delay for correction to the R.U.C. Station of the district where the holder resides.

X.   In no circumstances will reasons be given for a refusal either to grant or to renew a permit.

Ministry of Home Affairs,
      (Residence Permit Branch),
            Belfast.

W14700/365.5m.10/45.BL.G112—7261

Freda's Travel Documentation

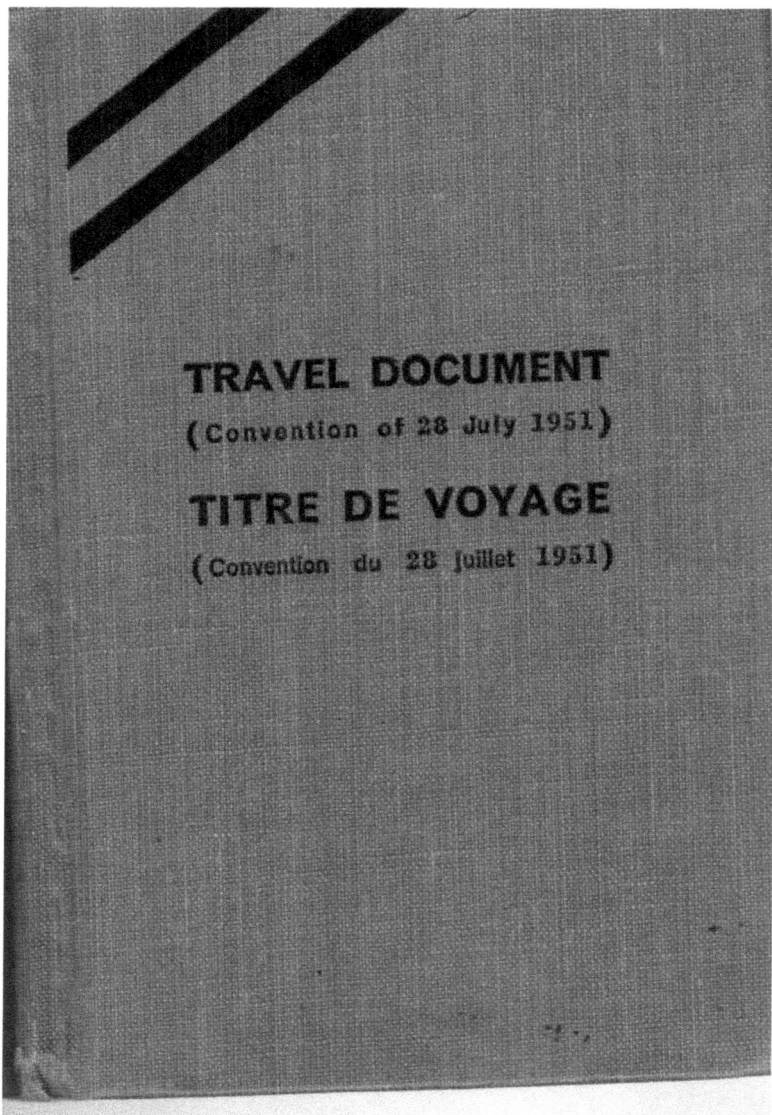

TRAVEL DOCUMENT
(Convention of 28 July 1951)

TITRE DE VOYAGE
(Convention du 28 Juillet 1951)

Place and date of birth / Lieu et date de naissance } GERMANY. 21. 12. 1925

Occupation / Profession } HOUSEWIFE

Country of Residence / Pays de Résidence } NORTHERN IRELAND

*Maiden name and forename(s) of wife / Nom (avant le mariage) et prénom(s) de l'épouse } SUGA SOPHIA

*Name and forename(s) of husband / Nom et prénom(s) du mari } QUIGLEY SAMUEL

DESCRIPTION — SIGNALEMENT

Height / Taille } 5 FEET 4 INCHES

Hair / Cheveux } DARK-BROWN

Colour of eyes / Couleur des yeux } HAZEL

Nose / Nez } STUBB

Shape of face / Forme du visage } ROUND

Complexion / Teint } FAIR

Special peculiarities / Signes particuliers } NONE

CHILDREN — ENFANTS			
Name / Nom	Forename(s) / Prénom(s)	Place and date of birth / Lieu et date de naissance	Sex / Sexe
QUIGLEY PAMELAH	CLARA		FEMALE
	CLOUGH		
	DOWN PATRICK		
	CO DOWN		

*Strike out whichever does not apply. / *Biffer la mention inutile.

This document contains 32 pages, exclusive of cover. / Ce titre contient 32 pages, non compris la couverture.

PHOTOGRAPH OF HOLDER AND STAMP OF ISSUING AUTHORITY

PHOTOGRAPHIE DU TITULAIRE ET CACHET L'AUTORITÉ QUI LIVRE LE TITRE

Signature of Holder — Signature du Titulaire

Sophia Quigley

Signature of holder / Signature du titulaire }

Issued at / Délivré à } LONDON   24 MAY 1967

Date }

Signature and stamp of authority issuing the document. / Signature et cachet de l'autorité qui délivre le titre.

Fee paid / Taxe perçue } £1

For H.M. Chief Inspector

This document contains 32 pages, exclusive of cover. / Ce titre contient 32 pages, non compris la couverture.

---

1. This document is valid for the following countries: / Ce titre est délivré pour les pays suivants:

ALL COUNTRIES

EXCEPT POLAND

2. Document or documents on the basis of which the present document is issued: / Document ou documents sur la base duquel ou desquels le présent titre est délivré:

3. This document expires on 24 MAY 1969 unless its validity is extended or renewed.

The holder is authorized to return to UNITED KINGDOM on or before 24 MAY 1969 unless some later date is hereafter specified. (The period during which the holder is allowed to return must be not less than three months.)

Ce document expire le _____ sauf prorogation de validité.

Le titulaire est autorisé à retourner au ROYAUME UNI jusqu'au _____ sauf mention ci-après d'une date ultérieure. (La période pendant laquelle le titulaire est autorisé à retourner ne doit pas être inférieure à trois mois.)

Note.—Unless otherwise stated, the renewal date applies both to the period of validity of the document and to the period within which the holder may return to the United Kingdom.

À moins de mention spéciale la date d'expiration de ce document est également celle de la date limite permettant le retour du titulaire dans le Royaume Uni.

This document contains 32 pages, exclusive of cover. / Ce titre contient 32 pages, non compris la couverture.

EXTENSION OR RENEWAL OF VALIDITY ★   PROROGATION DE VALIDITÉ

Fee paid / Taxe perçue:

From / du }
To / au }

Done at / Fait à }   Date / le }

Signature and stamp of authority extending or renewing the validity of the document.
Signature et cachet de l'autorité qui proroge la validité du titre.

EXTENSION OR RENEWAL OF VALIDITY ★   PROROGATION DE VALIDITÉ

Fee paid / Taxe perçue:

From / du }
To / au }

Done at / Fait à }   Date / le }

Signature and stamp of authority extending or renewing the validity of the document.
Signature et cachet de l'autorité qui proroge la validité du titre.

*See footnote on page 4. / *See footnote on page 4.

This document contains 32 pages, exclusive of cover. / Ce titre contient 32 pages, non compris la couverture.

Freda's Travel Permit

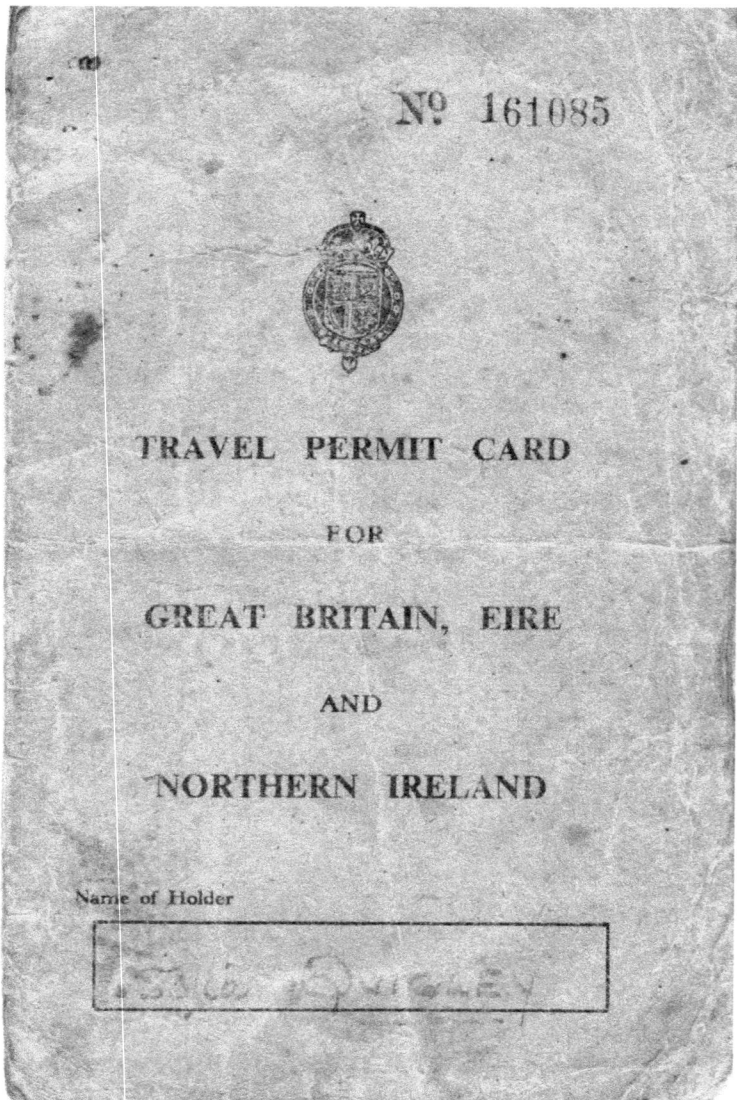

Nº 161085

TRAVEL PERMIT CARD

FOR

GREAT BRITAIN, EIRE

AND

NORTHERN IRELAND

Name of Holder

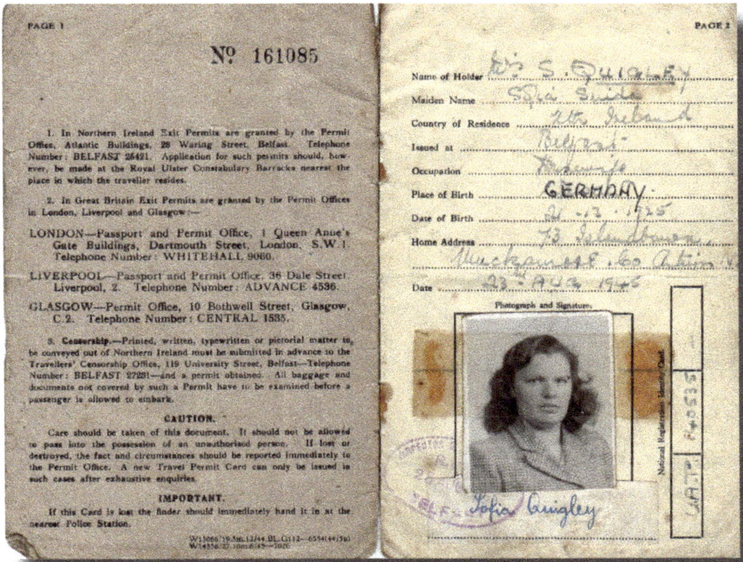

PAGE 1

№ 161085

1. In Northern Ireland Exit Permits are granted by the Permit Office, Atlantic Buildings, 28 Waring Street, Belfast. Telephone Number: BELFAST 25421. Application for such permits should, however, be made at the Royal Ulster Constabulary Barracks nearest the place in which the traveller resides.

2. In Great Britain Exit Permits are granted by the Permit Offices in London, Liverpool and Glasgow:—

LONDON—Passport and Permit Office, 1 Queen Anne's Gate Buildings, Dartmouth Street, London, S.W.1. Telephone Number: WHITEHALL 9060.

LIVERPOOL—Passport and Permit Office, 36 Dale Street, Liverpool, 2. Telephone Number: ADVANCE 4536.

GLASGOW—Permit Office, 10 Bothwell Street, Glasgow, C.2. Telephone Number: CENTRAL 1535.

3. **Censorship.**—Printed, written, typewritten or pictorial matter to be conveyed out of Northern Ireland must be submitted in advance to the Travellers' Censorship Office, 119 University Street, Belfast—Telephone Number: BELFAST 27281—and a permit obtained. All baggage and documents not covered by such a Permit have to be examined before a passenger is allowed to embark.

CAUTION.

Care should be taken of this document. It should not be allowed to pass into the possession of an unauthorised person. If lost or destroyed, the fact and circumstances should be reported immediately to the Permit Office. A new Travel Permit Card can only be issued in such cases after exhaustive enquiries.

IMPORTANT.

If this Card is lost the finder should immediately hand it in at the nearest Police Station.

PAGE 2

Name of Holder ....

Maiden Name ....

Country of Residence ....

Issued at .... Belfast

Occupation ....

Place of Birth .... GERMANY

Date of Birth ....

Home Address ....

Date .... 23 AUG 1945

Photograph and Signature.

Sofia Quigley

National Registration Identity Card

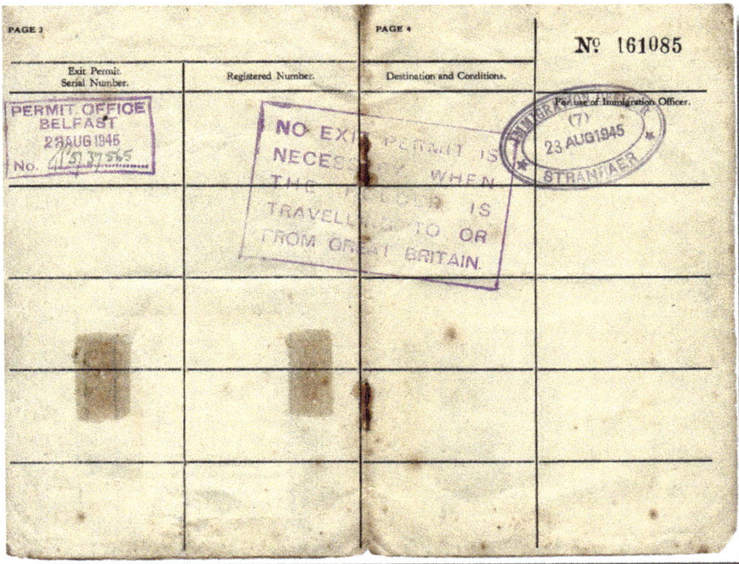

PAGE 3

PAGE 4

№ 161085

Exit Permit Serial Number.	Registered Number.	Destination and Conditions.	For use of Immigration Officer.
PERMIT OFFICE BELFAST 23 AUG 1945 No.	NO EXIT PERMIT IS NECESSARY WHEN THE HOLDER IS TRAVELLING TO OR FROM GREAT BRITAIN.		IMMIGRATION OFFICER (7) 23 AUG 1945 STRANRAER

Freda's Photo Gallery

Freda in her early years

Freda (in the middle) with her brother & sisters

Freda (on the right) with sisters & brother

Freda on the right with her brother & sisters

Freda during the war years

Freda with her first born, Terry

Sam, Freda & Family

**From right: Sam, Freda and friends
Toni and Tom Pyper**

**Family at Sam & Freda's Golden Wedding Anniversary
June 1995**

From right: Freda and her three sisters:
Anni, Mimi, Lotti.
Sam and his daughter Edith at back.

From right: Freda and her sister Mimi

**Sam and Freda at Sam's Imperial Service Medal
presentation**

Sam and Freda's Life in Colour

Freda during her war years

Freda in her early years

Freda (in the middle) with her brother and sisters

Freda (on the right) with her brother and sisters

Freda (on the right) with sisters and brother

Freda with her first born, Terry

Sam and Freda's family would like to thank you,
for reading their remarkable story.

Sam and Freda

A publication by Newford Publishing

www.newfordpublishing.com

www.ingramcontent.com/pod-product-compliance
Lightning Source LLC
Chambersburg PA
CBHW070821100426
42813CB00003B/436